■ SCHOLASTIC

100 Word-Building Pyramid Puzzles

Reproducible Word-Work Activities That Motivate Students to Practice and Strengthen Reading, Vocabulary, Spelling, and Phonics Skills

IMMACULA A. RHODES

D1361747

New York • Toronto • London • Auckland • Sydney
Mexico City • New Delhi • Hong Kong • Buenos Aires

Teaching Resources

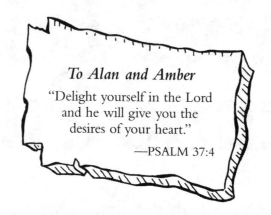

To Alan and Amber

"Delight yourself in the Lord
and he will give you the
desires of your heart."

—PSALM 37:4

Cover and interior design by Maria Lilja
Interior illustration by Teresa Anderko

ISBN: 978-0-545-20822-2

Text copyright © 2011 by Immacula A. Rhodes
Illustrations copyright © 2011 by Scholastic Inc.
Published by Scholastic Inc.
All rights reserved.
Printed in the U.S.A.

3 4 5 6 7 8 9 10   40   18 17 16 15 14 13 12 11

Contents

Introduction

Research shows that a strong foundation in phonics, recognition of spelling patterns, and knowing and using vocabulary-related strategies are important components in building comprehension and fluency. The unique design of the activities in *100 Word-Building Pyramid Puzzles* gets students actively engaged in analyzing words and practicing important skills that help strengthen both reading and writing. The game-like puzzles challenge students to think about the meaning, spelling, pronunciation, and use of words in context as they work their way up the pyramids to discover the final word at the top.

Much like the building blocks of a pyramid, the words that go up each side of these puzzles connect in a special way—either through shared letters or similar spelling patterns. Students explore words as they read clues on each side of the pyramid and then change, add, remove, or rearrange letters to create new words. After "climbing" both sides to the top, they use a clue and specific letters from previous words to decode the final, mystery word. The thought-provoking clues encourage students to analyze and think critically about words—the sound-symbol relationships in them, what they mean, their spelling and how the spelling relates to word meaning, their use in sentences, and how changing or moving letters affects pronunciation and meaning. Clues include definitions, antonyms, synonyms, examples, fill-in-the-blanks, and context clues to help students discover the correct words to put in the pyramids.

The self-checking format of the puzzles allows you to use them in any number of ways. They work well for small-group or whole-class lessons, independent or learning-center activities, day starters, activities for fast-finishers, and even for homework. The puzzles offer repeated practice in essential skills, making them ideal for use with struggling students, English Language Learners, and for RTI instruction.

Once students solve a few of these intriguing puzzles, they'll be hooked! The activities can be completed in about 10 minutes and are fun, motivating, and chock-full of opportunities to practice word skills. And best of all, students won't even realize how much they're learning when they do the puzzles!

Connections to the Language Arts Standards

The activities in this book are designed to support you in meeting national and state language arts standards. See page 7, for more.

Solving the Pyramid Puzzles

Students will enjoy solving the pyramid puzzles on their own. But, before they begin working independently, demonstrate how to solve a few puzzles to ensure they understand the steps and will succeed. As you work on the puzzles with students, you might use a think-aloud method to model strategies for using the clues to complete the puzzles.

1. To begin, students read the bottom word on one side of the pyramid. Then they look at the clue on the next step up. That clue gives a hint about the next word's meaning. It also tells whether to change, add, remove, or rearrange letters in the first word to come up with the next word. In the example at right, for instance, *a* is removed from *paint* to get the word *pint*.

2. Students work their way up the pyramid in this manner, one word at a time, until they've filled in the last word on that side. (Encourage them to check that each word makes sense and is spelled correctly before moving on to the next word.)

3. Once they complete one side of the pyramid, they use the clues to do the other side.

4. To find the final mystery word, students read the clue and look at the equation at the top. Then they combine letters from the last word on the left and right sides—using the equation as a guide—to discover the final word. For example, in the puzzle below, the final clue takes 2 letters from each word (*2 letters + 2 letters*). As an additional check, the letters that students should use will be underlined with bold lines.

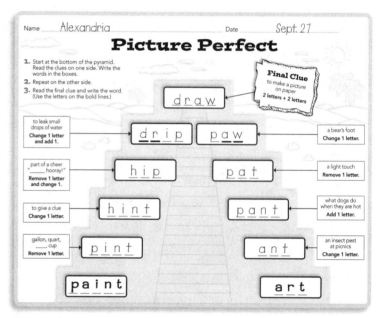

Tips for Working With the Puzzles

Try these quick and easy suggestions for using the puzzles and extending learning:

❋ Decide ahead of time whether you want to do the pyramid puzzles with the class as a whole, or have students work alone, in pairs, or in groups. Then choose a puzzle and make a copy for each student. For whole-class or small-group lessons, you might use an interactive whiteboard or overhead projector. If using the puzzles in a learning center, place them in a folder and have students remove one to complete during their visit to the center.

❋ At first, you may want to read the clues aloud to students, especially beginners. You might also provide additional clues, or elaborate on the meanings of words, to give students help with those that they find difficult.

❋ For extra support, list the "answers" for the puzzles in random order on the board or chart paper. Have students choose words from the list to complete the puzzle.

❋ If students get stuck on a particular word, you might tell them the word, then see if they can spell it correctly by making the appropriate changes in the previous word.

✳ After students solve the puzzles, encourage them to look at the two bottom words and the final word up at the top of the pyramid. Ask them to tell how these three words are connected to each other and to the puzzle title.

✳ Using a completed puzzle, point out that the final word gets its beginning consonant(s) from the last word on the left and a word-family ending from the last word on the right. Then invite students to brainstorm other words that share the same beginning letter (or letter combinations) or the same word-family ending with the final word.

✳ Have students sort words from the puzzles into various categories, such as words belonging to the same word family, words that begin with the same letter, nouns and verbs, short- and long-vowel words, or animal and object words. Doing this can help deepen students' understanding of word relationships.

✳ Try reversing the activity. To do this, fill in the answers on a puzzle and mask the clues. Copy the puzzle and distribute it to students. Then work with them to come up with their own clues for all of the words.

Connections to the Language Arts Standards

McREL Standards

Mid-continent Research for Education and Learning (McREL), a nationally recognized nonprofit organization, has compiled and evaluated national and state standards—and proposed what teachers should provide for their Grades 2–3 students to grow proficient in language arts, among other curriculum areas. The activities in this book support the following standards:

Reading

Uses the general skills and strategies of the reading process including:

- Uses basic elements of phonetic analysis (for example, common letter/sound relationships, beginning consonants, vowel sounds, blends, word patterns) to decode unknown words
- Uses basic elements of structural analysis (syllables and spelling patterns) to decode unknown words
- Understands level-appropriate sight words and vocabulary, including synonyms, antonyms, homophones, and multi-meaning words
- Uses context clues, definition, restatement, example, comparison and contrast to verify word meanings
- Uses self-correction strategies (searches for cues, identifies miscues, rereads)

Writing

Uses grammatical and mechanical conventions in written compositions including:

- Uses pronouns, nouns, verbs, adjectives, and adverbs in writing
- Uses conventions of spelling in writing (spells high frequency, commonly misspelled words from appropriate grade-level list; spells phonetically regular words; uses letter-sound relationships; spells basic short-vowel, long-vowel, r-controlled, and consonant-blend patterns; uses initial consonant substitution to spell related words; uses vowel combinations for correct spelling)

Source: Kendall, J. S., & Marzano, R. J. (2004). *Content knowledge: A compendium of standards and benchmarks for K–12 education.* Aurora, CO: Mid-continent Research for Education and Learning. Online database: http://www.mcrel. org/standards-benchmarks/

Common Core State Standards

The activities in this book also correlate with the English Language Arts standards recommended by the Common Core State Standards Initiative, a state-led effort to establish a single set of clear educational standards whose aim is to provide students with a high-equality education. At the time that this book went to press, these standards were still being finalized. To learn more, go to www.corestandards.org.

Furry Friends

1. Start at the bottom of the pyramid. Read the clues on one side. Write the words in the boxes.
2. Repeat on the other side.
3. Read the final clue and write the word. (Use the letters on the bold lines.)

Final Clue
a tame animal that people take care of
1 letter + 2 letters

Use this to catch a goldfish.
Change 1 letter.

Squirrels like to eat this.
Change 1 letter

Use a knife to do this.
Change 1 letter.

"a square ____ in a round hole"
Change 1 letter.

This helps hold up a table.
Change 1 letter.

wood that burns in a fireplace
Change 1 letter.

c a t

d o g

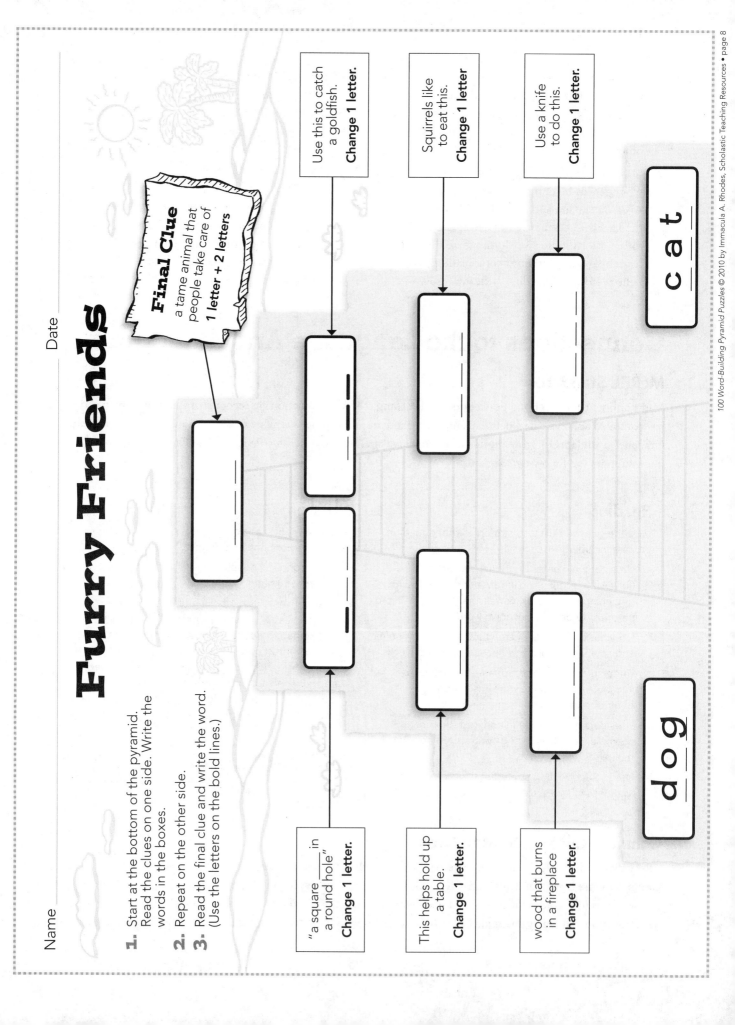

Name _____

Sweet Spread

1. Start at the bottom of the pyramid. Read the clues on one side. Write the words in the boxes.

2. Repeat on the other side.

3. Read the final clue and write the word. (Use the letters on the bold lines.)

Final Clue
the top that goes on a butter dish
1 letter + 2 letters

"I need to get ____ of this trash." **Change 1 letter.**

outer edge of a bowl **Change 1 letter.**

a male sheep **Change 1 letter.**

"I held the kitten in my ____." **Change 1 letter.**

the top of a soda bottle **Change 1 letter.**

Drive this on the road. **Change 1 letter.**

j a m

j a r

Name _____

Date _____

Catching Critters

1. Start at the bottom of the pyramid.
   Read the clues on one side. Write the
   words in the boxes.
2. Repeat on the other side.
3. Read the final clue and write the word.
   (Use the letters on the bold lines.)

Final Clue

Jelly is often put
in one of these.
1 letter + 2 letters

opposite of near
Change 1 letter.

"Let's get
a treat at the
snack ____."
Change 1 letter.

used for
carrying things
Change 1 letter.

b u g
_ _ _

a very fast airplane
Change 1 letter.

things that
belong together
a ____ of blocks
Change 1 letter.

"You can buy
a bird at the ____
store."
Change 1 letter.

n e t
_ _ _

Name _____

Date _____

Special Delivery

1. Start at the bottom of the pyramid. Read the clues on one side. Write the words in the boxes.

2. Repeat on the other side.

3. Read the final clue and write the word. (Use the letters on the bold lines.)

Final Clue

A letter carrier delivers this.

1 letter + 3 letters

Wind blows this to move a boat. **Change 1 letter.**

"Moo!" _____ the cow. **Change 1 letter.**

tiny grains that cover a beach **Change 1 letter.**

used to find your way to a new place "Look for Main Street on the _____." **Change 1 letter.**

a baseball player's hat **Remove 1 letter.**

to sleep outdoors in a tent **Remove 1 letter and change 1.**

s e n d

s t a m p

100 Word-Building Pyramid Puzzles © 2010 by Immacula A. Rhodes, Scholastic Teaching Resources • page 11

Name _____

Date _____

Made by Hand

1. Start at the bottom of the pyramid. Read the clues on one side. Write the words in the boxes.
2. Repeat on the other side.
3. Read the final clue and write the word. (Use the letters on the bold lines.)

Final Clue
to trim something
"I just got my hair ___."
1 letter + 2 letters

another word for stomach
Change 1 letter.

past tense of get
Remove 1 letter and change 1.

Rings are made of this yellow metal.
Change 1 letter.

f o l d
_ _ _ _

a baby bear
Remove 1 letter.

People become members of this.
"I joined a book ___."
Change 1 letter.

a hint
Change 1 letter.

g l u e
_ _ _ _

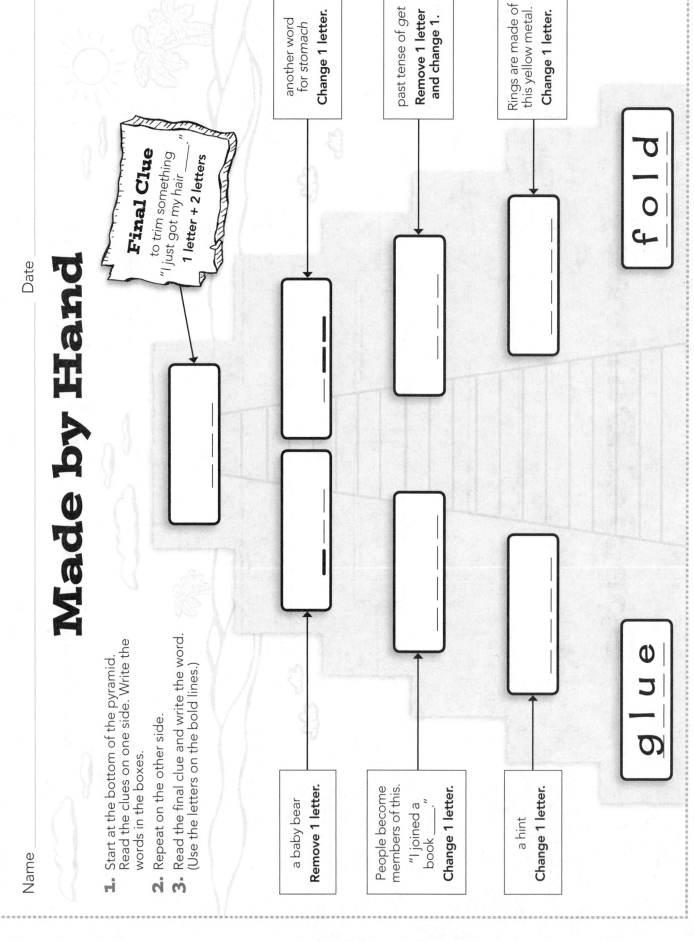

Name _____

Date _____

The Upper Level

1. Start at the bottom of the pyramid. Read the clues on one side. Write the words in the boxes.
2. Repeat on the other side.
3. Read the final clue and write the word. (Use the letters on the bold lines.)

Final Clue
This body part holds up your head.
1 letter + 3 letters

how birds get food from the ground
Change 1 letter.

the top of a mountain
Change 2 letters.

a bug that bothers you
Remove 1 letter and change 1.

c h e s t
_ _ _ _ _

opposite of far
Change 1 letter.

what you do with your ears
Change 1 letter.

to cure a sick person
Change 1 letter.

h e a d
_ _ _ _

Name _____

On the Water

1. Start at the bottom of the pyramid. Read the clues on one side. Write the words in the boxes.

2. Repeat on the other side.

3. Read the final clue and write the word. (Use the letters on the bold lines.)

Final Clue
to travel by boat
1 letter + 3 letters

to scoop water out of a leaky boat
Change 1 letter.

used on a hook when fishing
Add 1 letter.

a small, furry mammal that hangs upside down
Remove 1 letter.

to keep money in a bank
Change 1 letter.

a home for bats
Change 1 letter.

Birthday candles are put on this.
Change 1 letter.

b o a t

l a k e

Name _____

Date _____

A Nice Day Out

1. Start at the bottom of the pyramid. Read the clues on one side. Write the words in the boxes.
2. Repeat on the other side.
3. Read the final clue and write the word. (Use the letters on the bold lines.)

Final Clue
another word for *relax*
1 letter + 3 letters

good, better, _____
Change 1 letter.

past tense of *bend*
Change 1 letter.

"I must _____ down to tie my shoes."
Remove 1 letter and change 1.

not very common
"I found a _____ coin on the ground."
Change 1 letter.

not covered
"Her feet were _____."
Change 1 letter.

A dog makes this sound.
Change 1 letter.

b e n c h

p a r k

Going for a Walk

1. Start at the bottom of the pyramid. Read the clues on one side. Write the words in the boxes.
2. Repeat on the other side.
3. Read the final clue and write the word. (Use the letters on the bold lines.)

Final Clue

an outdoor area where people play and take walks

1 letter + 3 letters

the outer covering of a tree **Change 1 letter and rearrange letters.**	
to cook a pie in the oven **Change 1 letter.**	
short word for *bicycle* **Change 1 letter.**	

another word for *hurt* **Change 1 letter.**	
water that drops from the sky **Change 1 letter.**	
A train rides on this. **Remove 1 letter.**	

h i k e

t r a i l

Name _____

Date _____

Running Around

1. Start at the bottom of the pyramid. Read the clues on one side. Write the words in the boxes.
2. Repeat on the other side.
3. Read the final clue and write the word. (Use the letters on the bold lines.)

Final Clue
a small furry animal that likes cheese
1 letter + 4 letters

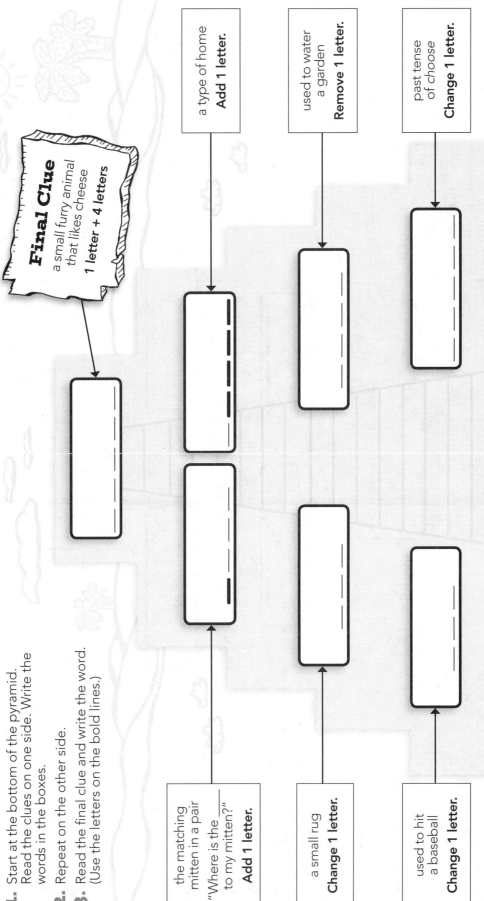

a type of home
Add 1 letter.

used to water a garden
Remove 1 letter.

past tense of choose
Change 1 letter.

the matching mitten in a pair
"Where is the _____ to my mitten?"
Add 1 letter.

a small rug
Change 1 letter.

used to hit a baseball
Change 1 letter.

c h a s e

c a t

At the Game

1. Start at the bottom of the pyramid.
   Read the clues on one side. Write the
   words in the boxes.
2. Repeat on the other side.
3. Read the final clue and write the word.
   (Use the letters on the bold lines.)

Final Clue

to throw a baseball
to a batter
1 letter + 4 letters

another word
for hook
"We'll ____ the
trailer to the car."
Change 1 letter.

how chicks leave
their eggs
Change 1 letter.

Use this to start
a fire.
Change 1 letter.

a kind of medicine
"Take one ____
at bedtime."
Change 1 letter.

a small mountain
Change 1 letter.

a long passage
between rooms
Change 1 letter.

c a t c h __

b a l l __

Name _____

Date _____

Little One

1. Start at the bottom of the pyramid. Read the clues on one side. Write the words in the boxes.
2. Repeat on the other side.
3. Read the final clue and write the word. (Use the letters on the bold lines.)

Final Clue
another word for *kid*
2 letters + 3 letters

opposite of tame
Change 1 letter.

"I hope you _____ come to my party."
Change 1 letter.

A fish breathes with this.
Change 1 letter.

to cut into small pieces
Change 1 letter and add 1.

the highest point of a hill
Change 1 letter.

something a child plays with
Change 1 letter.

g i r l

b o y

Name _____

Date _____

At the Door

1. Start at the bottom of the pyramid. Read the clues on one side. Write the words in the boxes.
2. Repeat on the other side.
3. Read the final clue and write the word. (Use the letters on the bold lines.)

Final Clue
the opposite of open
2 letters + 3 letters

a tube that water runs through
Change 1 letter and add 1.

opposite of cold
Change 1 letter.

a small house made of straw
Remove 1 letter.

Use this to hold papers together. "May I have a paper _____?"
Change 1 letter.

to fall down on a wet floor
Change 1 letter.

another word for *thin*
Change 1 letter.

s h u t
_ _ _ _

s l a m
_ _ _ _

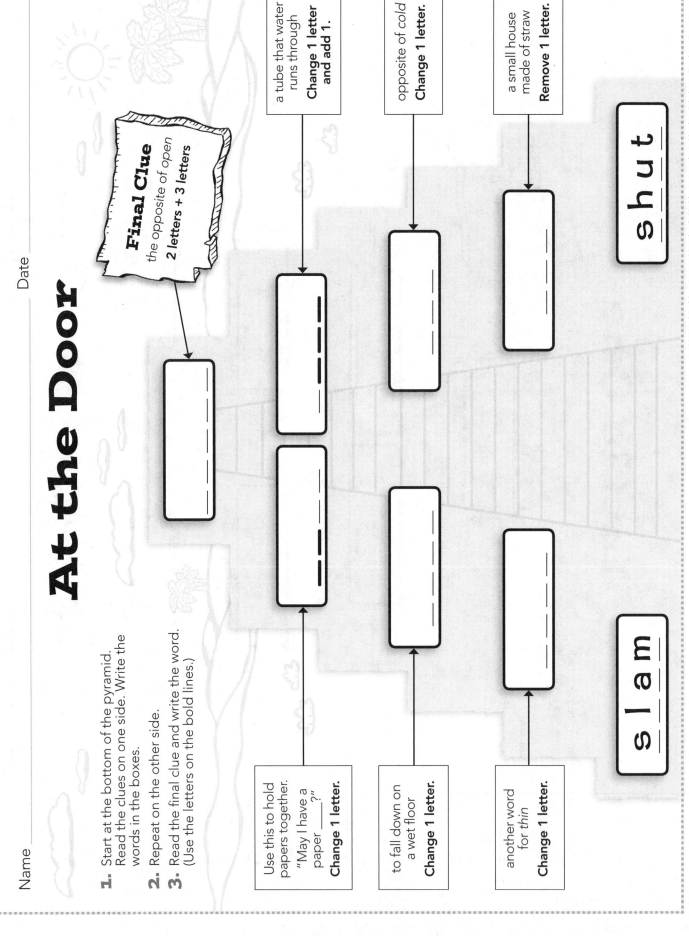

Fun Figures

1. Start at the bottom of the pyramid. Read the clues on one side. Write the words in the boxes.
2. Repeat on the other side.
3. Read the final clue and write the word. (Use the letters on the bold lines.)

Final Clue

a form, such as a circle or triangle
2 letters + 3 letters

sticky strip that holds two things together
Change 1 letter.

a cloak draped over the shoulders
"The superhero has a red ___."
Change 1 letter.

"I take ___ of my fish."
Remove 2 letters and change 1.

opposite of *he*
Change 1 letter and rearrange letters.

belonging to a girl
"This is ___ pencil."
Remove 1 letter.

to listen
Remove 1 letter.

s q u a r e
_ _ _ _ _ _

h e a r t
_ _ _ _ _

Name _____

Date _____

Colorful Words

1. Start at the bottom of the pyramid. Read the clues on one side. Write the words in the boxes.
2. Repeat on the other side.
3. Read the final clue and write the word. (Use the letters on the bold lines.)

Final Clue
the color of fresh grass
2 letters + 3 letters

"Have you ___ my new bike?"
Add 1 letter.

"I use my eyes to ___."
Change 1 letter.

a bug that buzzes and stings
Remove 1 letter and change 1.

past tense of *grow*
"The flower ___ fast!"
Change 1 letter and add 1.

opposite of *many*
Change 1 letter.

past tense of *feed*
"Have you ___ the dog?"
Change 1 letter.

b l u e

r e d

Name _____

Date _____

Underfoot

1. Start at the bottom of the pyramid. Read the clues on one side. Write the words in the boxes.
2. Repeat on the other side.
3. Read the final clue and write the word. (Use the letters on the bold lines.)

Final Clue

Grass grows on this.

2 letters + 4 letters

past tense of *find*
Change 1 letter and add 1.

a baseball that is hit out of bounds
Change 1 letter.

shiny silver wrap used in the kitchen
"I wrapped my sandwich in _____."
Change 1 letter.

to get taller
Change 1 letter.

a large black bird
Add 1 letter.

an oar is used to do this
Remove 1 letter and change 1.

s o i l

r o c k

Name _____

Date _____

Signs of the Season

1. Start at the bottom of the pyramid.
   Read the clues on one side. Write the words in the boxes.
2. Repeat on the other side.
3. Read the final clue and write the word. (Use the letters on the bold lines.)

Final Clue

to drop to the ground

1 letter + 3 letters

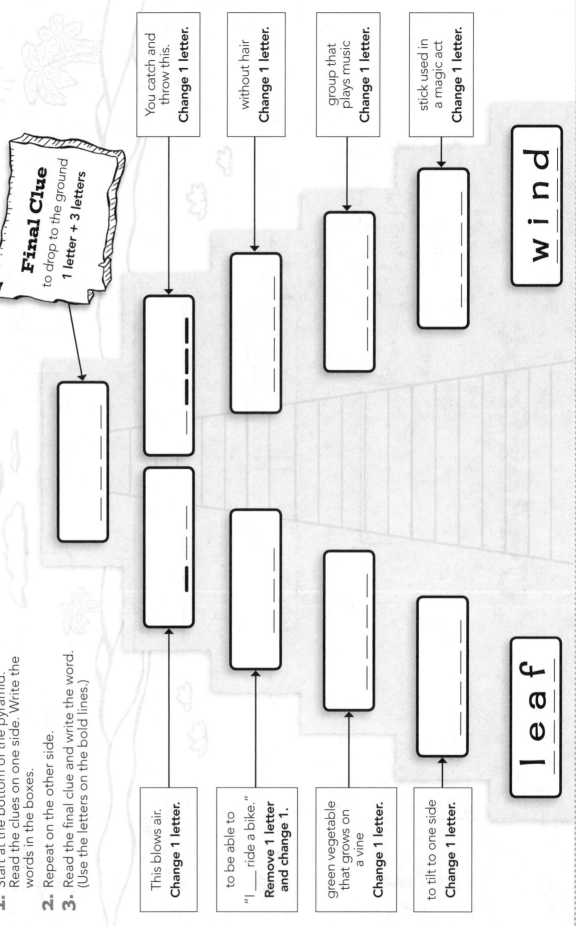

You catch and throw this. **Change 1 letter.**

without hair **Change 1 letter.**

group that plays music **Change 1 letter.**

stick used in a magic act **Change 1 letter.**

This blows air. **Change 1 letter.**

to be able to "I ____ ride a bike." **Remove 1 letter and change 1.**

green vegetable that grows on a vine **Change 1 letter.**

to tilt to one side **Change 1 letter.**

w i n d

l e a f

Name _____

Date _____

Coin Keeper

1. Start at the bottom of the pyramid. Read the clues on one side. Write the words in the boxes.
2. Repeat on the other side.
3. Read the final clue and write the word. (Use the letters on the bold lines.)

Final Clue
to put away for later
1 letter + 3 letters

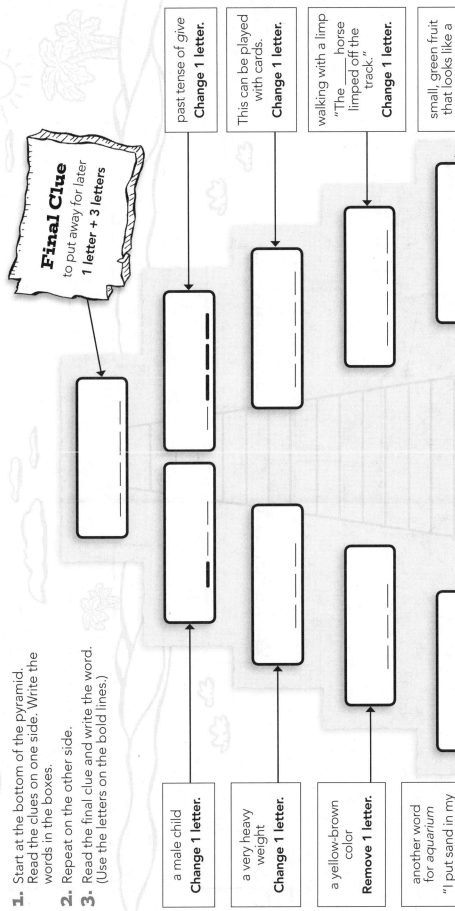

past tense of *give*
Change 1 letter.

This can be played with cards.
Change 1 letter.

walking with a limp
"The ____ horse limped off the track."
Change 1 letter.

small, green fruit that looks like a lemon
Change 1 letter.

a male child
Change 1 letter.

a very heavy weight
Change 1 letter.

a yellow-brown color
Remove 1 letter.

another word for aquarium
"I put sand in my fish ____."
Change 1 letter.

d i me

b a n k

Name _____

Date _____

A Great Story

1. Start at the bottom of the pyramid. Read the clues on one side. Write the words in the boxes.
2. Repeat on the other side.
3. Read the final clue and write the word. (Use the letters on the bold lines.)

Final Clue
to sound out words in a book
1 letter + 3 letters

Thread this on a string to make a necklace. **Change 1 letter.**

a bird's mouth **Change 1 letter.**

a small hole that lets water drip out **Change 2 letters.**

"I use my eyes to _____ around." **Change 1 letter.**

b o o k

a large mouse-like pest **Change 1 letter.**

a soft tap with the hand **Change 1 letter.**

a friend **Remove 1 letter.**

having a very light color **Change 1 letter.**

p a g e

On the Road

1. Start at the bottom of the pyramid. Read the clues on one side. Write the words in the boxes.
2. Repeat on the other side.
3. Read the final clue and write the word. (Use the letters on the bold lines.)

Final Clue

a journey

"We took a field ____ to the zoo."

2 letter + 2 letters

a bone at the top of your leg
Change 1 letter.

past tense of *hide*
Change 1 letter.

to offer a price for something
"We ____ on the painting."
Change 1 letter.

a very young flower
"The rose ____ will open soon."
Change 1 letter.

another word for garbage
Add 1 letter.

a red, itchy area on the skin
Change 1 letter and add 1.

a piece of old cloth
Change 1 letter.

This shows the price of something.
Change 1 letter.

bus

bag

Batter Up!

1. Start at the bottom of the pyramid. Read the clues on one side. Write the words in the boxes.
2. Repeat on the other side.
3. Read the final clue and write the word. (Use the letters on the bold lines.)

Final Clue

a ball player tags this with his foot

1 letter + 3 letters

"Pack your suit ____ for the trip."
Change 1 letter.

"Help me put icing on the ____."
Change 1 letter.

not real
Change 2 letters.

another name for *autumn*
Change 1 letter.

b	a l l __

This has two wheels and handlebars.
Change 1 letter.

the same as another thing
Change 1 letter.

not dead
Change 1 letter.

opposite of *hate*
Remove 1 letter.

g l o v e

Name _____   Date _____

Let's Go Out!

1. Start at the bottom of the pyramid. Read the clues on one side. Write the words in the boxes.
2. Repeat on the other side.
3. Read the final clue and write the word. (Use the letters on the bold lines.)

Final Clue
Wear this outside to stay warm on a cold day.

1 letter + 3 letters

People travel across water in this. **Add 1 letter.**

Cereal can be made of this grain. **Change 1 letter.**

another word for a boat paddle **Change 1 letter.**

This has four tires and a steering wheel. **Remove 2 letters.**

to heat food in a pan **Change 1 letter.**

People read this. **Change 1 letter.**

Fish bait is put on this. **Change 1 letter.**

sound made by an owl **Change 1 letter.**

scarf

boot

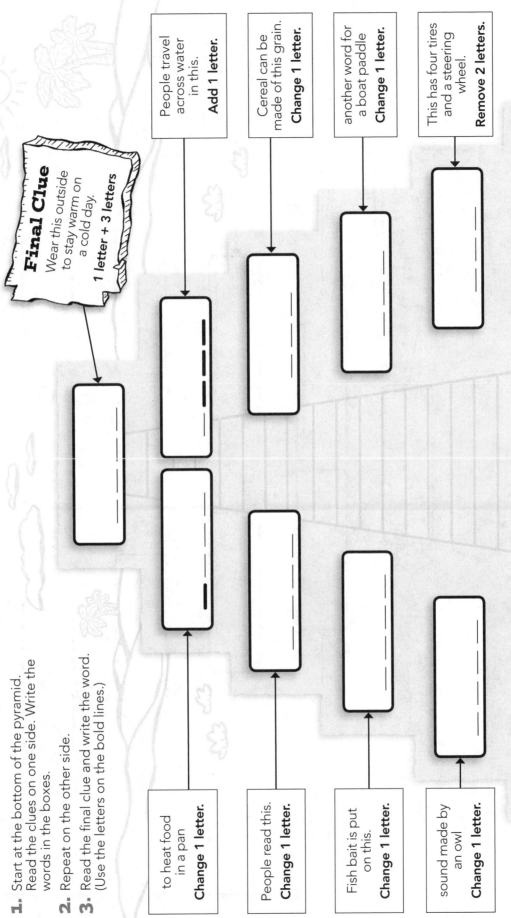

Name _____

Date _____

Flapping and Flying

1. Start at the bottom of the pyramid. Read the clues on one side. Write the words in the boxes.
2. Repeat on the other side.
3. Read the final clue and write the word. (Use the letters on the bold lines.)

Final Clue
do this with your hand when saying "Goodbye"
1 letter + 3 letters

past tense of *give*
Change 1 letter.

Workers do this to a road.
Change 1 letter.

part of a book
Change 1 letter.

without much color
Change 1 letter.

fake hair
Change 1 letter.

opposite of *little*
Change 1 letter.

a paper or plastic sack
Change 1 letter.

to fall behind others in a line
Remove 1 letter.

p o l e

f l a g

Put It on Paper

1. Start at the bottom of the pyramid. Read the clues on one side. Write the words in the boxes.
2. Repeat on the other side.
3. Read the final clue and write the word. (Use the letters on the bold lines.)

Final Clue
to make words
on paper
2 letters + 3 letters

a toy that flies
in the wind
Add 1 letter.

"There's a needle
in my sewing
_____."
Change 1 letter.

the seed inside
a peach
Change 1 letter.

a type of jewelry
Change 1 letter.

p e n

opposite of *right*
**Change 1 letter
and add 1.**

another word
for *tune*
Change 1 letter.

past tense of *sing*
Change 1 letter.

used to make
castles at the
beach
Change 1 letter.

h a n d

Name _____

Date _____

On the Go!

1. Start at the bottom of the pyramid. Read the clues on one side. Write the words in the boxes.
2. Repeat on the other side.
3. Read the final clue and write the word. (Use the letters on the bold lines.)

Final Clue
to push something from one place to another
1 letter + 3 letters

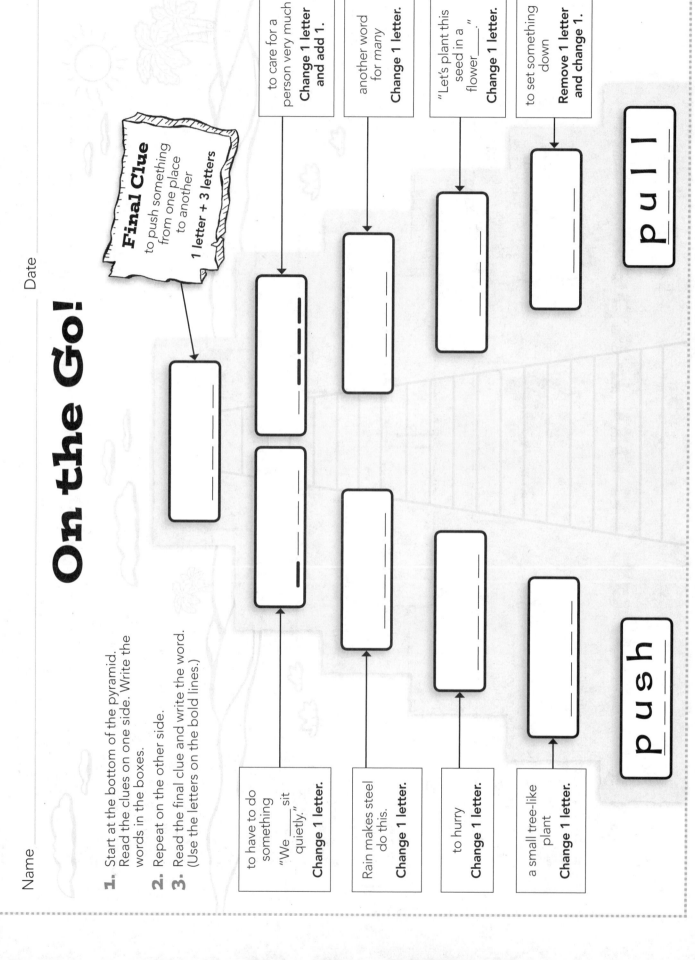

to care for a person very much
Change 1 letter and add 1.

another word for many
Change 1 letter.

"Let's plant this seed in a flower ____."
Change 1 letter.

to set something down
Remove 1 letter and change 1.

p u l l

to have to do something
"We ____ sit quietly."
Change 1 letter.

Rain makes steel do this.
Change 1 letter.

to hurry
Change 1 letter.

a small tree-like plant
Change 1 letter.

p u s h

Name _____

On Your Feet

1. Start at the bottom of the pyramid.
   Read the clues on one side. Write the words in the boxes.
2. Repeat on the other side.
3. Read the final clue and write the word. (Use the letters on the bold lines.)

Final Clue
opposite of *sit*
2 letters + 3 letters

This has fingers and a thumb. **Change 1 letter.**

to put a picture on a wall **Change 1 letter.**

"I got to school before the bell ____." **Add 1 letter.**

past tense of run **Change 1 letter.**

r u n

opposite of *fresh* "The bread is ____." **Add 1 letter.**

a type of story **Change 1 letter.**

very high **Change 1 letter.**

This divides one room from another. **Change 1 letter.**

w a l k

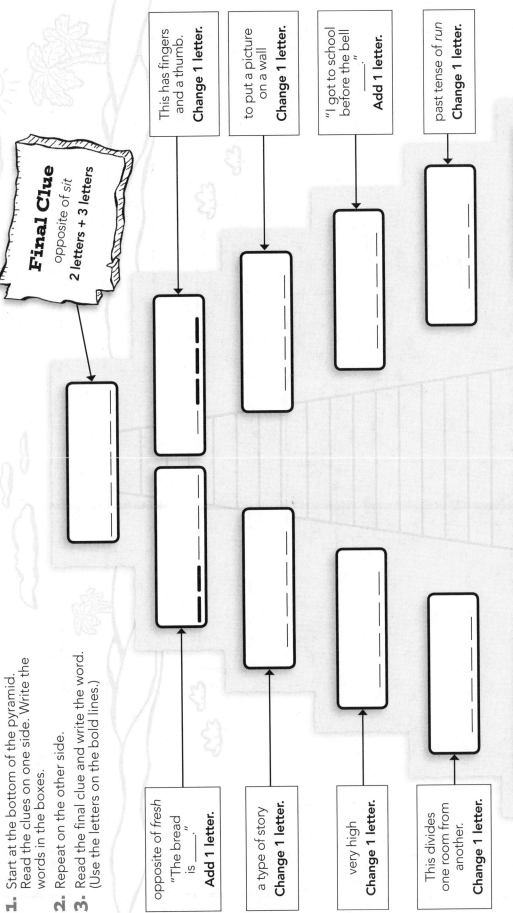

Name _____ Date _____

Shade Maker

1. Start at the bottom of the pyramid. Read the clues on one side. Write the words in the boxes.
2. Repeat on the other side.
3. Read the final clue and write the word. (Use the letters on the bold lines.)

Final Clue
a tall plant with a trunk and leaves
2 letters + 2 letters

a flying bug that stings
Change 1 letter.

a place to sleep
Remove 1 letter.

a small ball with a hole in the center
Change 1 letter.

to walk in the front of a line
Change 1 letter.

l e a f

This is used to catch a mouse.
Change 1 letter and add 1.

one full time around a track
Remove 1 letter.

A light bulb is put in this.
Change 1 letter.

a baby sheep
Change 1 letter.

l i m b

In the Water

1. Start at the bottom of the pyramid. Read the clues on one side. Write the words in the boxes.
2. Repeat on the other side.
3. Read the final clue and write the word. (Use the letters on the bold lines.)

Final Clue
how fish move through water
2 letters + 2 letters

not very bright
"The light in here is very ____."
Remove 1 letter and change 1.

the knob on a car radio
Change 1 letter.

to get a good price on something
Change 1 letter.

a water animal that has flippers
Add 1 letter.

s e a

to grow larger
"My bee sting ____ began to ____."
Add 1 letter.

not sick
Change 1 letter.

"Which shoes ____ you wear to school?"
Change 2 letters.

to hope something will happen
Change 1 letter.

f i s h

Name _____

Date _____

Living in the Wild

1. Start at the bottom of the pyramid. Read the clues on one side. Write the words in the boxes.

2. Repeat on the other side.

3. Read the final clue and write the word. (Use the letters on the bold lines.)

Final Clue
a large furry animal that lives in a den
1 letter + 3 letters

a drop of water that falls from your eye **Add 1 letter.**

sticky, black stuff that covers a road **Change 1 letter.**

You park this in a garage. **Remove 1 letter.**

to look after a person or pet **Change 1 letter.**

c a v e

another word for *insect* **Change 1 letter.**

a mat on the floor **Change 1 letter.**

to pull at gently **Change 1 letter.**

where people take a bath **Change 1 letter.**

c u b

Name _____

Date _____

Sun Up, Sun Down

1. Start at the bottom of the pyramid. Read the clues on one side. Write the words in the boxes.
2. Repeat on the other side.
3. Read the final clue and write the word. (Use the letters on the bold lines.)

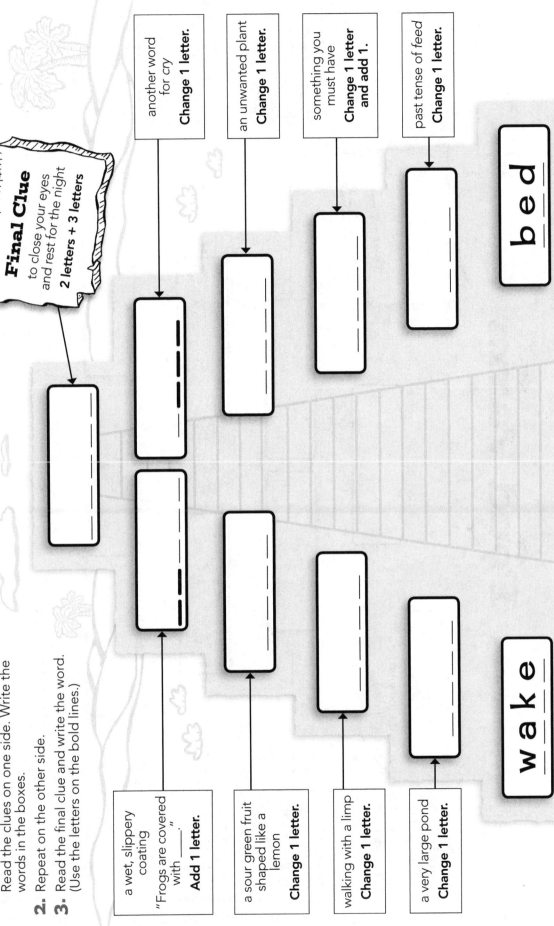

Final Clue
to close your eyes and rest for the night
2 letters + 3 letters

another word for cry
Change 1 letter.

an unwanted plant
Change 1 letter.

something you must have
Change 1 letter and add 1.

past tense of feed
Change 1 letter.

a wet, slippery coating
"Frogs are covered with _____."
Add 1 letter.

a sour green fruit shaped like a lemon
Change 1 letter.

walking with a limp
Change 1 letter.

a very large pond
Change 1 letter.

b e d

w a k e

Name _____

Date _____

Food Farm

1. Start at the bottom of the pyramid. Read the clues on one side. Write the words in the boxes.
2. Repeat on the other side.
3. Read the final clue and write the word. (Use the letters on the bold lines.)

Final Clue
what a farmer grows and harvests
2 letters + 2 letters

the highest part
"The bird flew to the _____ of the tree."
Change 1 letter.

An elephant weighs this much or more.
Remove 1 letter.

to have a rip
"My pants are _____."
Change 1 letter.

When a baby comes into the world, it is _____.
Change 1 letter.

c o r n

another word for *crawl*
Change 1 letter and add 1.

the sound of a horn
Change 1 letter.

a red vegetable that grows underground
Change 1 letter.

the sound of a drum
Change 1 letter.

b e a n

Name _____

Date _____

Fun With a Friend

1. Start at the bottom of the pyramid.
   Read the clues on one side. Write the
   words in the boxes.
2. Repeat on the other side.
3. Read the final clue and write the word.
   (Use the letters on the bold lines.)

Final Clue
to do something
for fun with a friend
2 letters + 2 letters

present tense
of said
Change 2 letters.

a young male
**Remove 1 letter
and change 1.**

"Your birthday
is the day you
were ___."
Change 1 letter.

to be on fire
Change 1 letter.

Food is served
on this.
Add 1 letter.

opposite of early
Change 1 letter.

the day of the
month
Change 1 letter.

a doorway in
a fence
Change 1 letter.

t u r n
___ ___ ___ ___

g a m e
___ ___ ___ ___

Name _____

Date _____

Up We Go!

1. Start at the bottom of the pyramid. Read the clues on one side. Write the words in the boxes.
2. Repeat on the other side.
3. Read the final clue and write the word. (Use the letters on the bold lines.)

Final Clue
another word for step
2 letters + 3 letters

done by the rules without cheating
Change 1 letter.

opposite of pass
"I hope I don't ___ the test."
Change 1 letter.

A dog wags this.
Change 1 letter.

to glide on water in a boat
Change 1 letter.

Stick this on a letter to mail it.
Change 1 letter and add 1.

Turn this on to light up a room.
Change 1 letter.

to walk with a stiff or hurt leg
Change 1 letter.

another word for *branch*
Remove 1 letter.

r a i l

c l i m b

Name _____

Date _____

In the Flowerpot

1. Start at the bottom of the pyramid. Read the clues on one side. Write the words in the boxes.
2. Repeat on the other side.
3. Read the final clue and write the word. (Use the letters on the bold lines.)

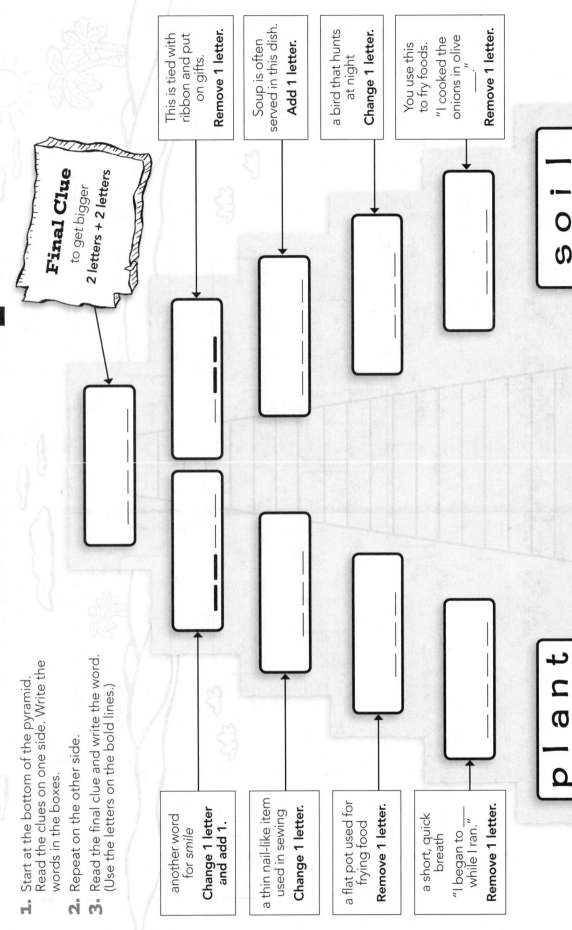

Final Clue
to get bigger
2 letters + 2 letters

This is tied with ribbon and put on gifts. **Remove 1 letter.**

Soup is often served in this dish. **Add 1 letter.**

a bird that hunts at night **Change 1 letter.**

You use this to fry foods. "I cooked the onions in olive ____." **Remove 1 letter.**

another word for *smile* **Change 1 letter and add 1.**

a thin nail-like item used in sewing **Change 1 letter.**

a flat pot used for frying food **Remove 1 letter.**

a short, quick breath "I began to ____ while I ran." **Remove 1 letter.**

s o i l

p l a n t

Name _____

Date _____

At the Store

1. Start at the bottom of the pyramid. Read the clues on one side. Write the words in the boxes.
2. Repeat on the other side.
3. Read the final clue and write the word. (Use the letters on the bold lines.)

Final Clue
to pay money for something
2 letters + 3 letters

to put a curve in something "Don't ____ the coat hanger." **Add 1 letter.**

Pillows and blankets go on this. **Change 1 letter.**

to ask for something over and over **Change 1 letter.**

a fly or ant **Change 1 letter.**

another word for stain **Add 1 letter.**

a pan used for cooking soup **Change 1 letter.**

a small round mark **Change 1 letter.**

a small bed **Remove 1 letter and change 1.**

b u y

c o i n

Hungry Hound

1. Start at the bottom of the pyramid. Read the clues on one side. Write the words in the boxes.
2. Repeat on the other side.
3. Read the final clue and write the word. (Use the letters on the bold lines.)

Final Clue
an animal that barks and digs holes
1 letter + 2 letters

a large pig **Change 1 letter.**

to wrap your arms around someone "Give your grandma a _____!" **Change 2 letters.**

"Put the trash in this plastic _____." **Change 1 letter.**

to keep someone out **Remove 1 letter.**

a wild lion lives in this **Change ___ letter.**

A person has this many toes. **Change 1 letter.**

2,000 pounds **Remove 1 letter.**

a musical sound **Change 1 letter.**

b a r k

b o n e

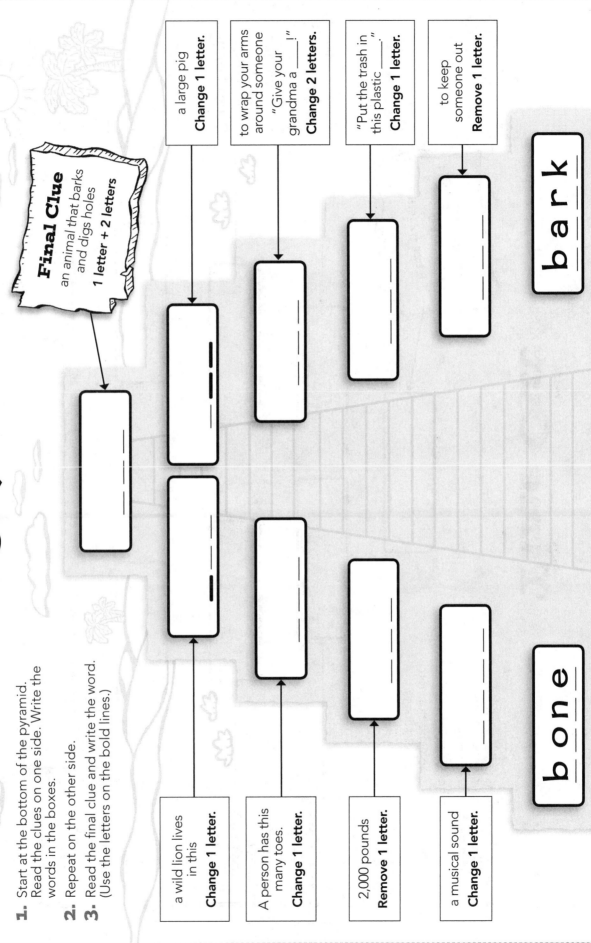

Name _____

Date _____

Time Out

1. Start at the bottom of the pyramid. Read the clues on one side. Write the words in the boxes.
2. Repeat on the other side.
3. Read the final clue and write the word. (Use the letters on the bold lines.)

Final Clue
a small, folding bed
1 letter + 2 letters

how a fire feels
Change 1 letter.

another word for *jump*
Change 1 letter.

used to clean up a spill on the floor
Change 1 letter.

a paper that shows roads and cities
Change 1 letter.

Use scissors to do this to paper.
Change 1 letter.

except
"I like all nuts _____ cashews."
Change 1 letter.

to take a risk on something
"I _____ our team will win."
Remove 1 letter.

the greatest of all
Change 1 letter.

n a p

r e s t

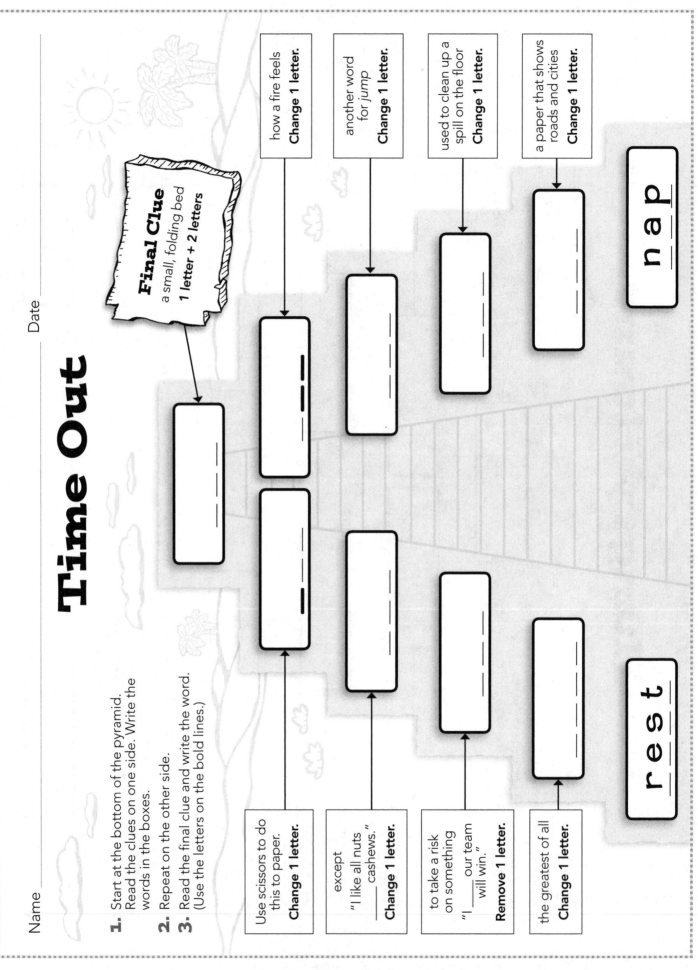

Name _____

Date _____

Tree Topper

1. Start at the bottom of the pyramid. Read the clues on one side. Write the words in the boxes.
2. Repeat on the other side.
3. Read the final clue and write the word. (Use the letters on the bold lines.)

Final Clue
where a bird lays its eggs
1 letter + 3 letters

the most liked
"I like my red shoes ____." **Change 1 letter.**

a strap worn around the waist **Change 1 letter.**

past tense of *feel* **Change 1 letter and add 1.**

the price paid to join a club **Remove 1 letter and change 1.**

t r e e

the number after *eight* **Change 1 letter.**

something that belongs to me **Change 1 letter.**

to care about something "Do you ____ if I come in?" **Change 1 letter.**

to fasten things together "Use a stapler to ____ the pages together." **Change 1 letter.**

b i r d

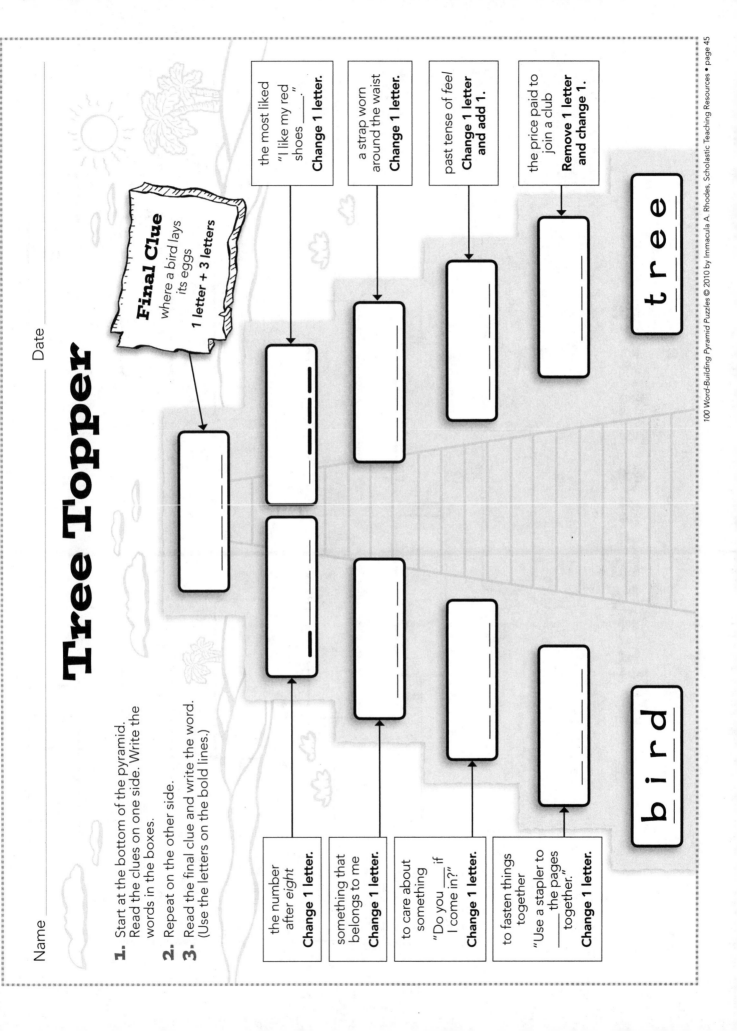

Name _____

Date _____

Chugging Along

1. Start at the bottom of the pyramid. Read the clues on one side. Write the words in the boxes.
2. Repeat on the other side.
3. Read the final clue and write the word. (Use the letters on the bold lines.)

Final Clue
the rails that a train rides on
2 letters + 3 letters

to fill a suitcase with clothes
Change 1 letter and add 1.

Eggs are fried in this.
Change 1 letter.

"The cat ____ away from the dog."
Remove 1 letter.

drops of water that fall from the sky
Remove 1 letter.

t r a i n

another word for journey
Add 1 letter.

another word for tear
Change 1 letter.

to get free of something
"We finally got ____ of the ants."
Remove 1 letter.

to take something quickly
"I think I'll ____ the cookie jar!"
Change 1 letter.

r a i l

Name _____

Check the Calendar

1. Start at the bottom of the pyramid. Read the clues on one side. Write the words in the boxes.
2. Repeat on the other side.
3. Read the final clue and write the word. (Use the letters on the bold lines.)

Final Clue
365 days make one of these.
1 letter + 3 letters

a short distance away
Change 1 letter.

word used to start a letter
Change 1 letter.

opposite of *alive*
Add 1 letter.

another word for *father*
Change 1 letter.

d a y

by now
"Is it snowing ____?"
Change 1 letter.

opposite of *dry*
Change 1 letter.

another word for *tiny*
Remove 1 letter.

plant that grows where it's not wanted
Change 1 letter.

w e e k

Name _____ Date _____

Say "Cheese!"

1. Start at the bottom of the pyramid. Read the clues on one side. Write the words in the boxes.

2. Repeat on the other side.

3. Read the final clue and write the word. (Use the letters on the bold lines.)

Final Clue
another word for *grin*
2 letters + 3 letters

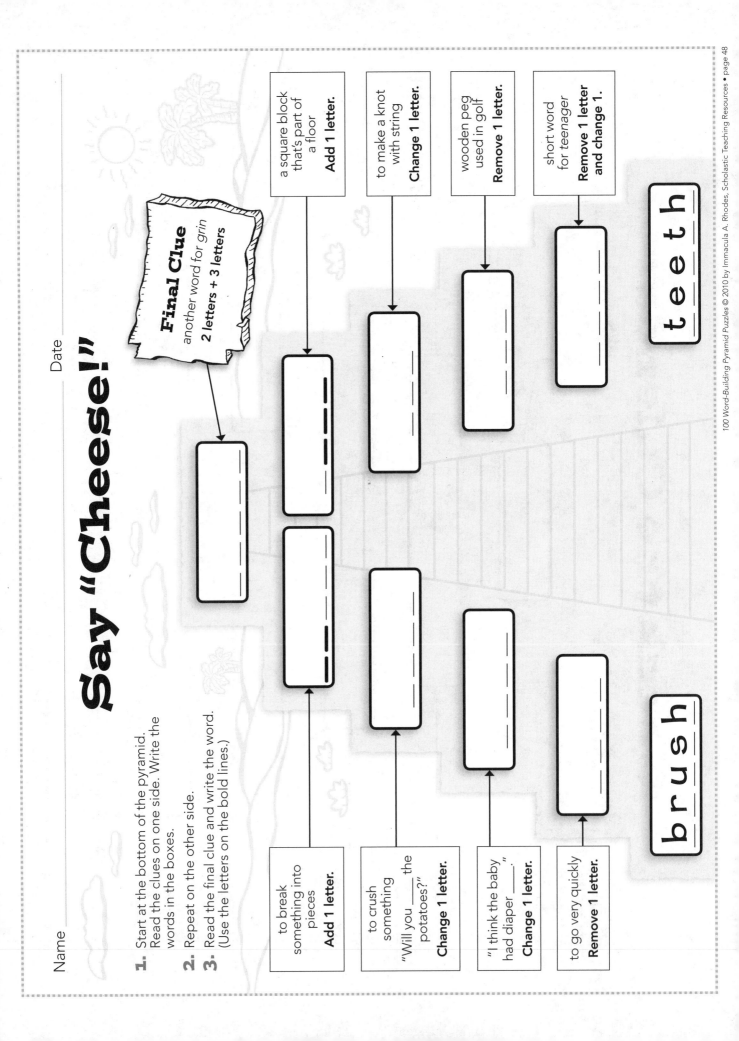

a square block that's part of a floor **Add 1 letter.**

to make a knot with string **Change 1 letter.**

wooden peg used in golf **Remove 1 letter.**

short word for teenager **Remove 1 letter and change 1.**

t e e t h

to break something into pieces **Add 1 letter.**

to crush something "Will you ____ the potatoes?" **Change 1 letter.**

"I think the baby had diaper ____." **Change 1 letter.**

to go very quickly **Remove 1 letter.**

b r u s h

Spending the Day Away

1. Start at the bottom of the pyramid. Read the clues on one side. Write the words in the boxes.

2. Repeat on the other side.

3. Read the final clue and write the word. (Use the letters on the bold lines.)

Final Clue
a large building full of stores
1 letter + 3 letters

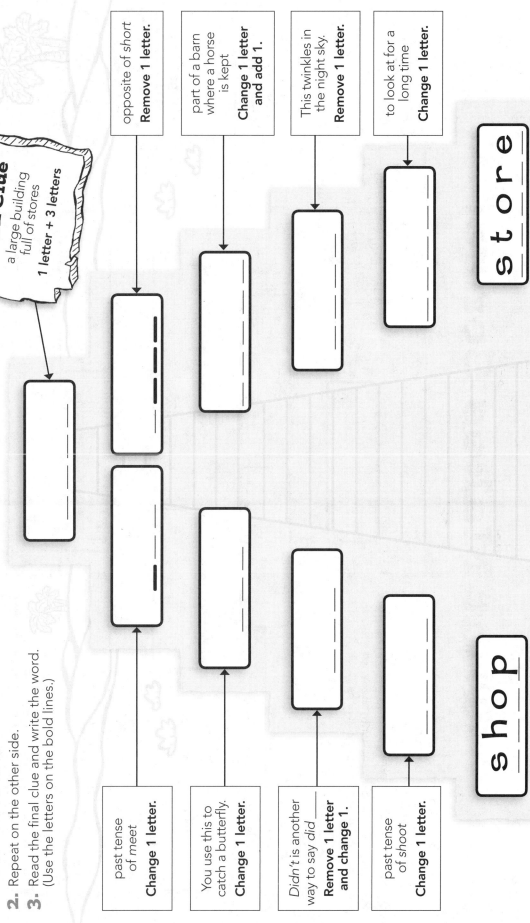

opposite of *short*
Remove 1 letter.

part of a barn where a horse is kept
Change 1 letter and add 1.

This twinkles in the night sky.
Remove 1 letter.

to look at for a long time
Change 1 letter.

s t o r e

past tense of *meet*
Change 1 letter.

You use this to catch a butterfly.
Change 1 letter.

Didn't is another way to say *did* _____
Remove 1 letter and change 1.

past tense of *shoot*
Change 1 letter.

s h o p

Name _____

Date _____

That Makes Sense!

1. Start at the bottom of the pyramid. Read the clues on one side. Write the words in the boxes.
2. Repeat on the other side.
3. Read the final clue and write the word. (Use the letters on the bold lines.)

Final Clue
You use your nose to do this.
2 letters + 3 letters

another word for *healthy*
Change 1 letter.

a place to hang pictures
Change 1 letter and add 1.

past tense of *is* "He ___ tired after the race."
Remove 2 letters.

to use more of something than you need
Change 1 letter.

t a s t e

knowing a lot of things
Change 1 letter.

another word for *begin*
Add 1 letter.

a famous person
Change 1 letter and add 1.

This body part is used for hearing.
Remove 1 letter.

h e a r

Name ____________________ Date ____________

Scrub-a-Dub-Dub

1. Start at the bottom of the pyramid. Read the clues on one side. Write the words in the boxes.
2. Repeat on the other side.
3. Read the final clue and write the word. (Use the letters on the bold lines.)

Final Clue
body part used for writing
1 letter + 3 letters

_ _ _ _

Left side	Right side
You wear this on your head. **Change 1 letter.** _ _ _	This covers most deserts. **Change 2 letters.** _ _ _ _
a small rug in front of a door "We put out a welcome ____." **Remove 1 letter.** _ _ _	another word for *bag* **Change 1 letter.** _ _ _ _
a post that holds a ship's sail **Change 1 letter.** _ _ _ _	This is worn on your foot. **Change 1 letter.** _ _ _ _
another word for *crush* "I helped Dad ____ the potatoes." **Change 1 letter.** _ _ _ _	to make very wet **Change 1 letter.** _ _ _ _
w a s h	s o a p

Name _____

Date _____

Look-Alikes

1. Start at the bottom of the pyramid. Read the clues on one side. Write the words in the boxes.
2. Repeat on the other side.
3. Read the final clue and write the word. (Use the letters on the bold lines.)

Final Clue
something that looks just like another thing
1 letter + 4 letters

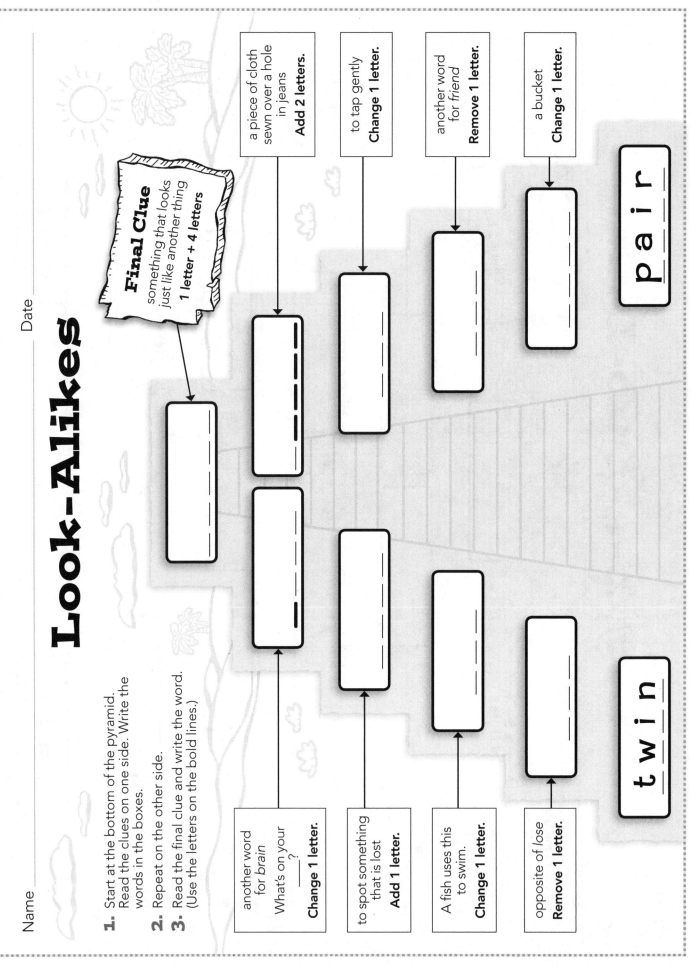

a piece of cloth sewn over a hole in jeans
Add 2 letters.

to tap gently
Change 1 letter.

another word for *friend*
Remove 1 letter.

a bucket
Change 1 letter.

p a i r

another word for *brain*
What's on your ____?
Change 1 letter.

to spot something that is lost
Add 1 letter.

A fish uses this to swim.
Change 1 letter.

opposite of *lose*
Remove 1 letter.

t w i n

Name _____   Date _____

Time to Cook

1. Start at the bottom of the pyramid.
   Read the clues on one side. Write the
   words in the boxes.
2. Repeat on the other side.
3. Read the final clue and write the word.
   (Use the letters on the bold lines.)

Final Clue
to mix things together
2 letters + 3 letters

to mail a letter
to someone
**Change 1 letter
and add 1.**

to get a table
ready for a meal
Change 1 letter.

opposite of *stand*
Change 1 letter.

number that
comes after *five*
Change 1 letter.

lose blood
from a cut
**Change 2 letters
and add 1.**

to leak out
"Water began to
___ ___ through the
crack."
Remove 1 letter.

a sharp slope
"We climbed the
___ ___ hill."
Change 1 letter.

to turn a car to
the left or right
**Change 1 letter
and add 1.**

m i x

s t i r

Name _____

Date _____

Dark to Light

1. Start at the bottom of the pyramid. Read the clues on one side. Write the words in the boxes.
2. Repeat on the other side.
3. Read the final clue and write the word. (Use the letters on the bold lines.)

Final Clue
the color of snow
2 letters + 3 letters

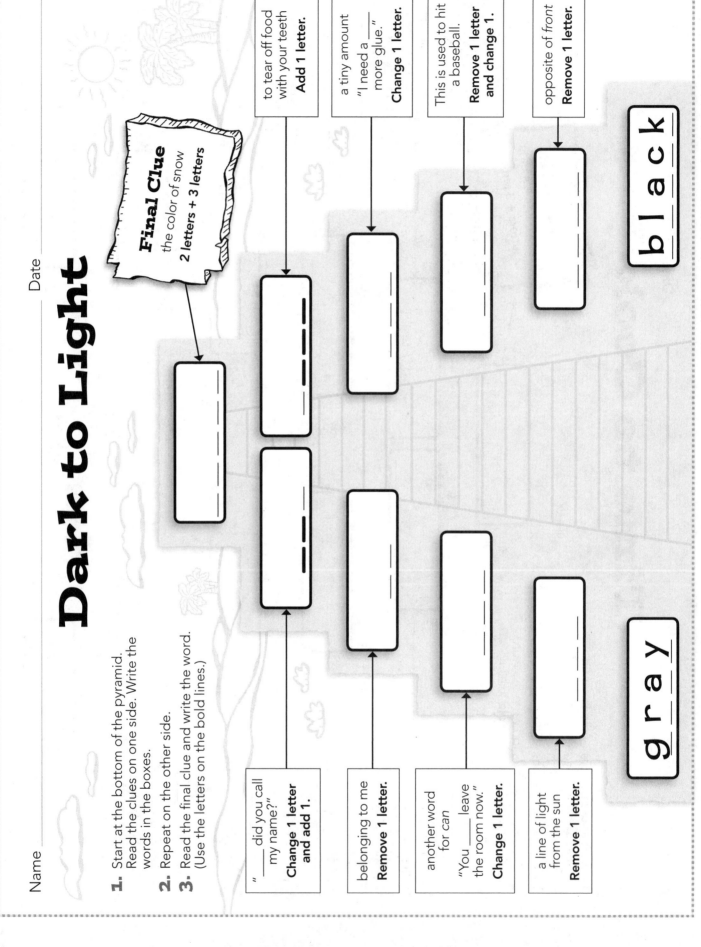

to tear off food with your teeth
Add 1 letter.

a tiny amount
"I need a ____ more glue."
Change 1 letter.

This is used to hit a baseball.
Remove 1 letter and change 1.

opposite of front
Remove 1 letter.

b l a c k

" ____ did you call my name?"
Change 1 letter and add 1.

belonging to me
Remove 1 letter.

another word for can
"You ____ leave the room now."
Change 1 letter.

a line of light from the sun
Remove 1 letter.

g r a y

Name _____

Date _____

Frozen Fun

1. Start at the bottom of the pyramid. Read the clues on one side. Write the words in the boxes.
2. Repeat on the other side.
3. Read the final clue and write the word. (Use the letters on the bold lines.)

Final Clue
to move across ice on boots that have blades
2 letters + 3 letters

another word for speed
"The nurse checked my heart _____"
Change 1 letter.

a contest to see who runs the fastest
Change 1 letter.

a white grain used for food
Change 1 letter.

more than one mouse
Add 1 letter.

i c e

the outer covering of your body
Add 1 letter.

family or relatives
Change 1 letter.

to come in first place
Remove 1 letter and change 1.

opposite of narrow
Remove 1 letter and change 1.

g l i d e

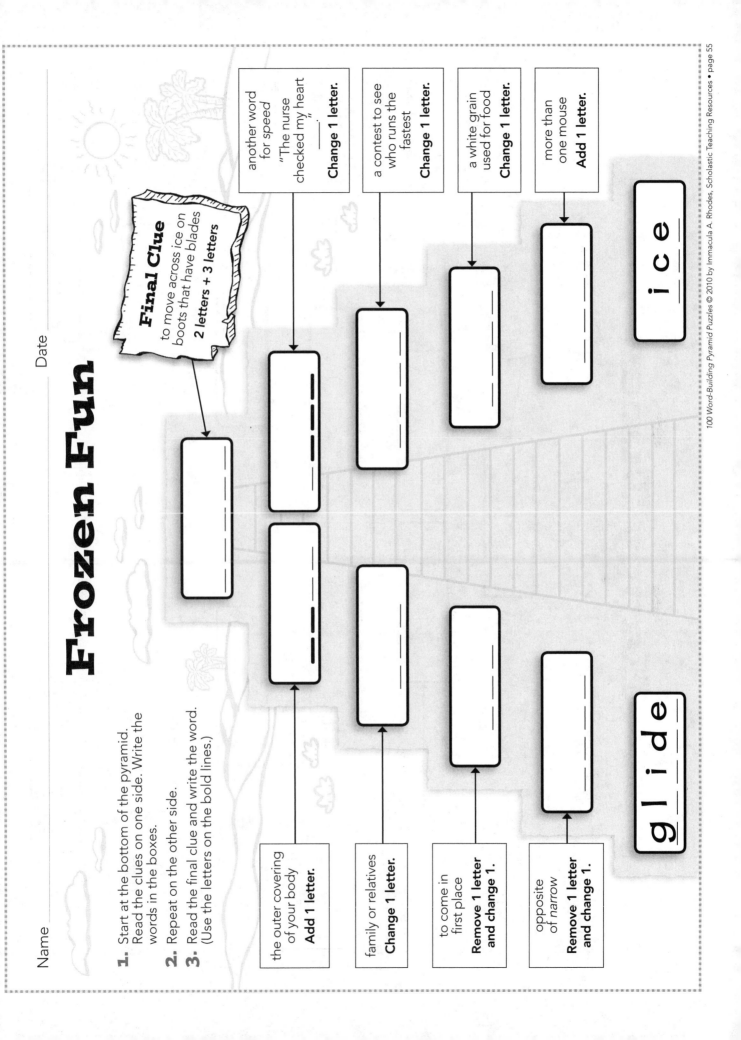

Name _____

Date _____

Happy Times

1. Start at the bottom of the pyramid. Read the clues on one side. Write the words in the boxes.
2. Repeat on the other side.
3. Read the final clue and write the word. (Use the letters on the bold lines.)

Final Clue
another word for happy
2 letters + 2 letters

another word for angry
Remove 1 letter.

past tense of make
Change 1 letter.

another word for man
Change 1 letter.

unit of measure for how far a car goes
Remove 1 letter.

s m i l e

another word for paste
Change 1 letter.

the color of the sky
Change 2 letters.

"_____ out the candles on the cake."
Change 2 letters.

to get taller and older
Change 2 letters.

g r i n

Name _____

Date _____

Surprise!

1. Start at the bottom of the pyramid.
   Read the clues on one side. Write the
   words in the boxes.
2. Repeat on the other side.
3. Read the final clue and write the word.
   (Use the letters on the bold lines.)

Final Clue

another word
for present

1 letter + 3 letters

to pick up
something heavy
Change 1 letter.

to write down
things to buy at
the store
Add 1 letter.

past tense of *light*
"Dad ___ the
candles on the
cake."
Change 1 letter.

the rim of a cup
Change 1 letter.

a long dress
Change 1 letter.

a small city
Add 1 letter.

to pull something
with a chain
Change 1 letter.

You tie your
shoelaces into one
of these.
Change 1 letter.

l i d

b o x

Name _____

Date _____

Squirrel's Lunch

1. Start at the bottom of the pyramid. Read the clues on one side. Write the words in the boxes.
2. Repeat on the other side.
3. Read the final clue and write the word. (Use the letters on the bold lines.)

Final Clue
the hard case around a walnut
2 letters + 3 letters

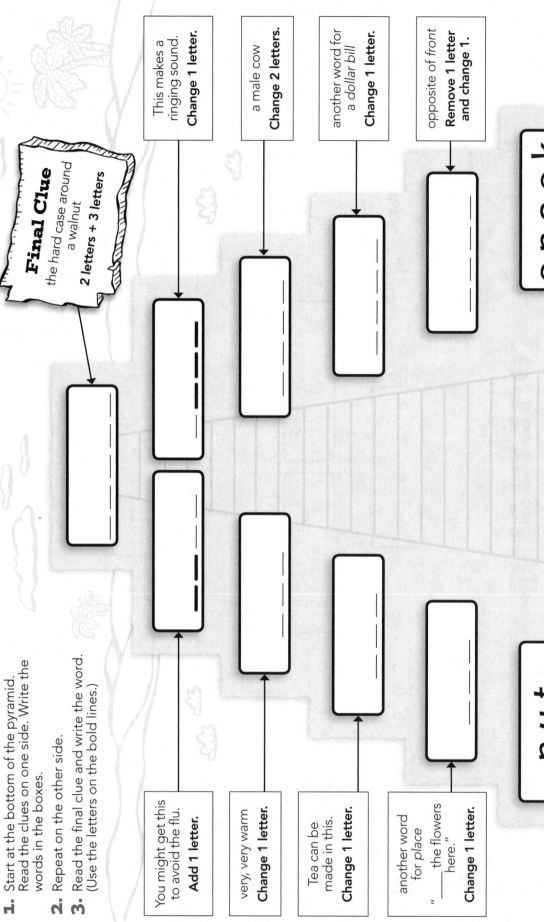

This makes a ringing sound. **Change 1 letter.**

a male cow **Change 2 letters.**

another word for a dollar bill **Change 1 letter.**

opposite of *front* **Remove 1 letter and change 1.**

c r a c k

You might get this to avoid the flu. **Add 1 letter.**

very, very warm **Change 1 letter.**

Tea can be made in this. **Change 1 letter.**

another word for place
"_____ the flowers here." **Change 1 letter.**

n u t

Name _____

Date _____

Mmm, Mmm, Good!

1. Start at the bottom of the pyramid. Read the clues on one side. Write the words in the boxes.
2. Repeat on the other side.
3. Read the final clue and write the word. (Use the letters on the bold lines.)

Final Clue
to heat water until it bubbles

1 letter + 3 letters

a silver sheet used for wrapping food **Change 1 letter.**

another word for gross "The trash has a ____ smell!" **Change 1 letter.**

This comes after *three.* **Change 1 letter.**

how a lemon tastes **Change 1 letter.**

better than all others "You are my ____ friend." **Change 1 letter.**

a person who bothers you **Change 1 letter.**

opposite of *present* **Change 1 letter.**

a pole used to hold up a fence **Add 1 letter.**

s o u p

p o t

Name _____

Date _____

Wet Weather

1. Start at the bottom of the pyramid. Read the clues on one side. Write the words in the boxes.
2. Repeat on the other side.
3. Read the final clue and write the word. (Use the letters on the bold lines.)

Final Clue
another word for shower
1 letter + 3 letters

an unwanted spot on a rug
Change 1 letter.

another word for a step
Remove 1 letter and add 1.

to look long and hard at
Change 1 letter.

You can buy clothes here.
Change 1 letter.

s	t	o	r	m

People drive cars on this.
Change 1 letter.

a frog-like animal with bumpy skin
Change 1 letter.

a lot
"He has a ___ of wood on the truck."
Change 1 letter.

opposite of quiet
Remove 1 letter.

c	l	o	u	d

Name _____

Date _____

Under Construction

1. Start at the bottom of the pyramid. Read the clues on one side. Write the words in the boxes.
2. Repeat on the other side.
3. Read the final clue and write the word. (Use the letters on the bold lines.)

Final Clue
a hammer is used to pound this into wood
1 letter + 3 letters

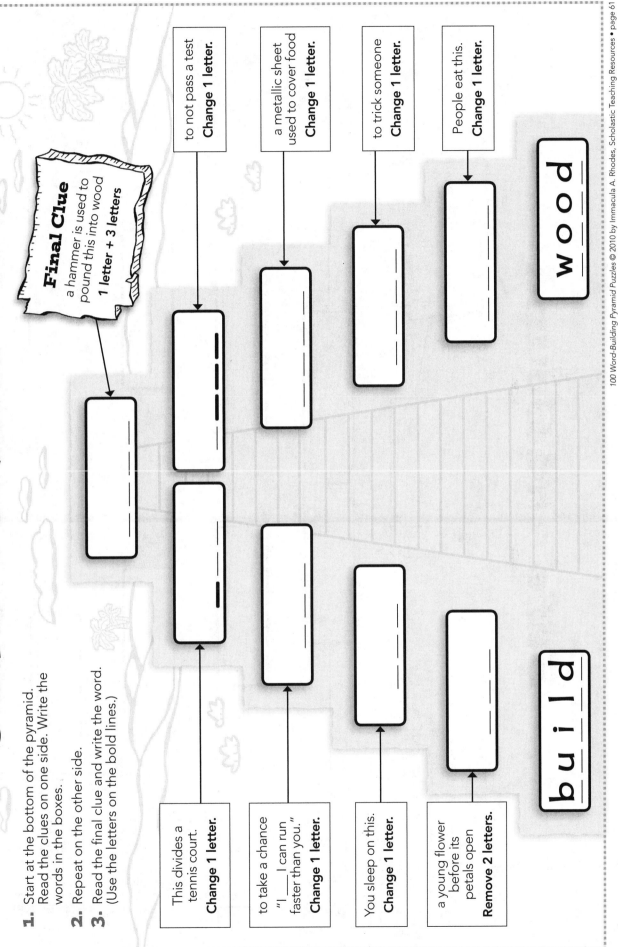

to not pass a test
Change 1 letter.

a metallic sheet used to cover food
Change 1 letter.

to trick someone
Change 1 letter.

People eat this.
Change 1 letter.

This divides a tennis court.
Change 1 letter.

to take a chance
"I ____ I can run faster than you."
Change 1 letter.

You sleep on this.
Change 1 letter.

a young flower before its petals open
Remove 2 letters.

w o o d

b u i l d

Name _____

Safe and Sound

1. Start at the bottom of the pyramid.
   Read the clues on one side. Write the words in the boxes.
2. Repeat on the other side.
3. Read the final clue and write the word. (Use the letters on the bold lines.)

Final Clue

another word for bolt

"Did you _____ the door?"

1 letter + 3 letters

A clock goes "tick-____."
Change 2 letters.

a hammer or wrench
Change 1 letter.

People swim in this.
Change 1 letter.

opposite of *rich*
Change 1 letter.

Science experiments are done here.
Change 1 letter.

another word for taxi
Remove 1 letter.

This beach animal has a shell and claws.
Change 1 letter and add 1.

to shed tears from your eyes
Change 2 letters.

d o o r

k e y

Breakin' Out

1. Start at the bottom of the pyramid. Read the clues on one side. Write the words in the boxes.
2. Repeat on the other side.
3. Read the final clue and write the word. (Use the letters on the bold lines.)

Final Clue
a baby bird
2 letters + 3 letters

opposite of healthy
Change 1 letter.

a bag used for groceries
Change 1 letter.

another word for rear
"You can sit in the ____ seat."
Change 1 letter.

a place to put dishes to dry
Remove 1 letter.

the lower part of your jaw
Change 1 letter and add 1.

to fasten a medal to a shirt
Change 1 letter.

another name for a hog
Change 1 letter.

A golf tee is a wooden ____.
Change 1 letter and rearrange letters.

c r a c k

e g g

Name ____________________ Date ____________

Size It Up

1. Start at the bottom of the pyramid. Read the clues on one side. Write the words in the boxes.
2. Repeat on the other side.
3. Read the final clue and write the word. (Use the letters on the bold lines.)

Final Clue
fully open
"He left the door ____ open."
1 letter + 3 letters

___ ___ ___ ___

Left side		Right side
a stick used in a magic act **Change 1 letter.**	___ ___ ___ ___ / ___ ___ ___ ___	"At high ____, the waves cover the beach." **Change 1 letter.**
a large area of ground **Change 1 letter.**	___ ___ ___ ___ / ___ ___ ___ ___	Check for this on a clock. **Change 1 letter.**
the name for a kind of road **Change 1 letter.**	___ ___ ___ ___ / ___ ___ ___ ___	to train a wild animal **Change 1 letter.**
short word for *alone* **Change 1 letter.**	___ ___ ___ ___ / ___ ___ ___ ___	a made-up story **Change 1 letter.**
	l o n g / t a l l	

Name _____

Date _____

Picture Perfect

1. Start at the bottom of the pyramid. Read the clues on one side. Write the words in the boxes.
2. Repeat on the other side.
3. Read the final clue and write the word. (Use the letters on the bold lines.)

Final Clue
to make a picture on paper
2 letters + 2 letters

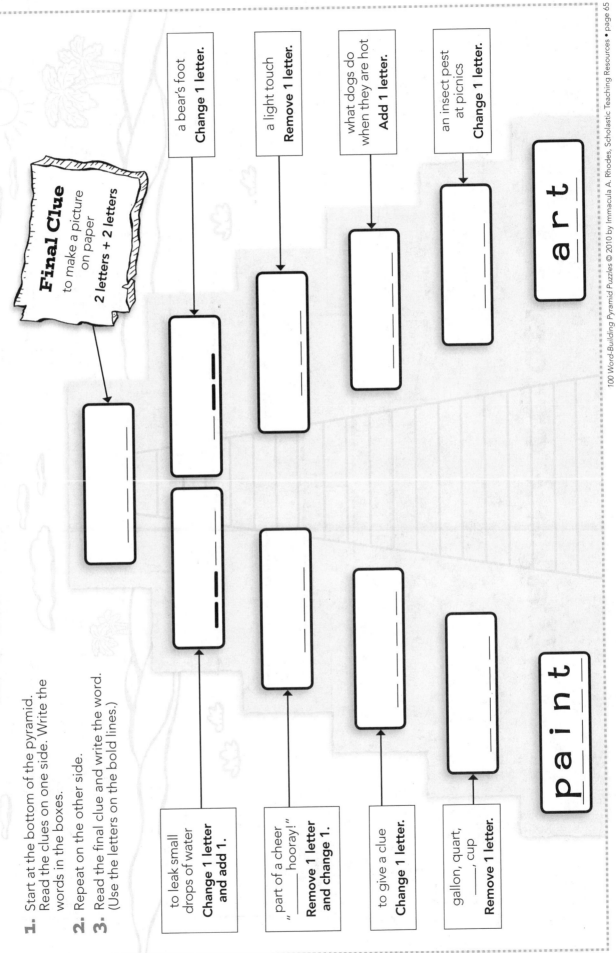

a bear's foot
Change 1 letter.

a light touch
Remove 1 letter.

what dogs do when they are hot
Add 1 letter.

an insect pest at picnics
Change 1 letter.

to leak small drops of water
Change 1 letter and add 1.

part of a cheer "_____, hooray!"
Remove 1 letter and change 1.

to give a clue
Change 1 letter.

gallon, quart, _____, cup
Remove 1 letter.

a r t

p a i n t

Name _____

Date _____

Take Action

1. Start at the bottom of the pyramid. Read the clues on one side. Write the words in the boxes.
2. Repeat on the other side.
3. Read the final clue and write the word. (Use the letters on the bold lines.)

Final Clue
very fast
2 letters + 3 letters

A dog does this with its tongue.
Change 1 letter and rearrange letters.

the same as "Your coat is _____ mine."
Change 1 letter.

the opposite of *die*
Change 1 letter.

to like something very much
Change 1 letter.

m o v e

to leave a job
Change 1 letter and add 1.

past tense of *light*
Change 1 letter.

a small piece of land
Change 1 letter.

opposite of *high*
Remove 1 letter.

s l o w

Name _____

Date _____

At the Seashore

1. Start at the bottom of the pyramid. Read the clues on one side. Write the words in the boxes.
2. Repeat on the other side.
3. Read the final clue and write the word. (Use the letters on the bold lines.)

Final Clue
a sandy shore by the ocean
1 letter + 4 letters

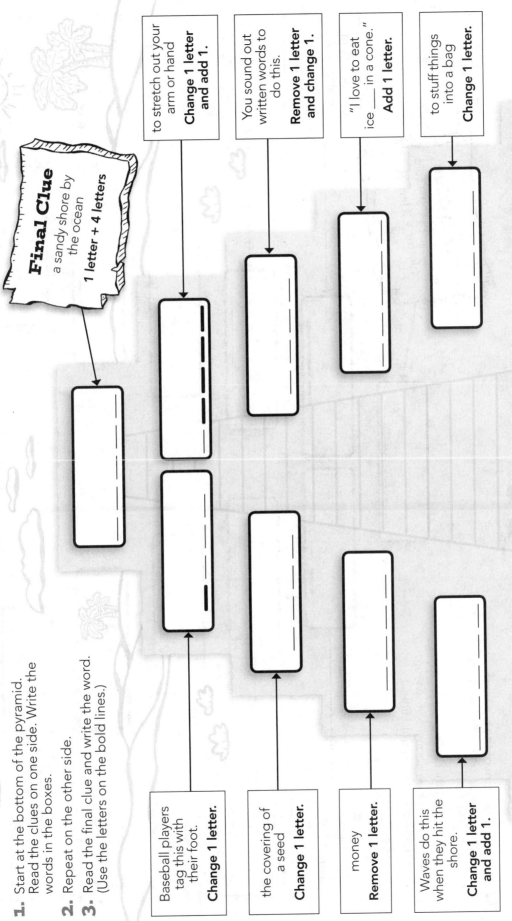

to stretch out your arm or hand
Change 1 letter and add 1.

You sound out written words to do this.
Remove 1 letter and change 1.

"I love to eat ice ____ in a cone."
Add 1 letter.

to stuff things into a bag
Change 1 letter.

Baseball players tag this with their foot.
Change 1 letter.

the covering of a seed
Change 1 letter.

money
Remove 1 letter.

Waves do this when they hit the shore.
Change 1 letter and add 1.

c l a m

c r a b

Name _____

Date _____

Steppin' Out

1. Start at the bottom of the pyramid. Read the clues on one side. Write the words in the boxes.
2. Repeat on the other side.
3. Read the final clue and write the word. (Use the letters on the bold lines.)

Final Clue
has a heel and a sole
1 letter + 3 letters

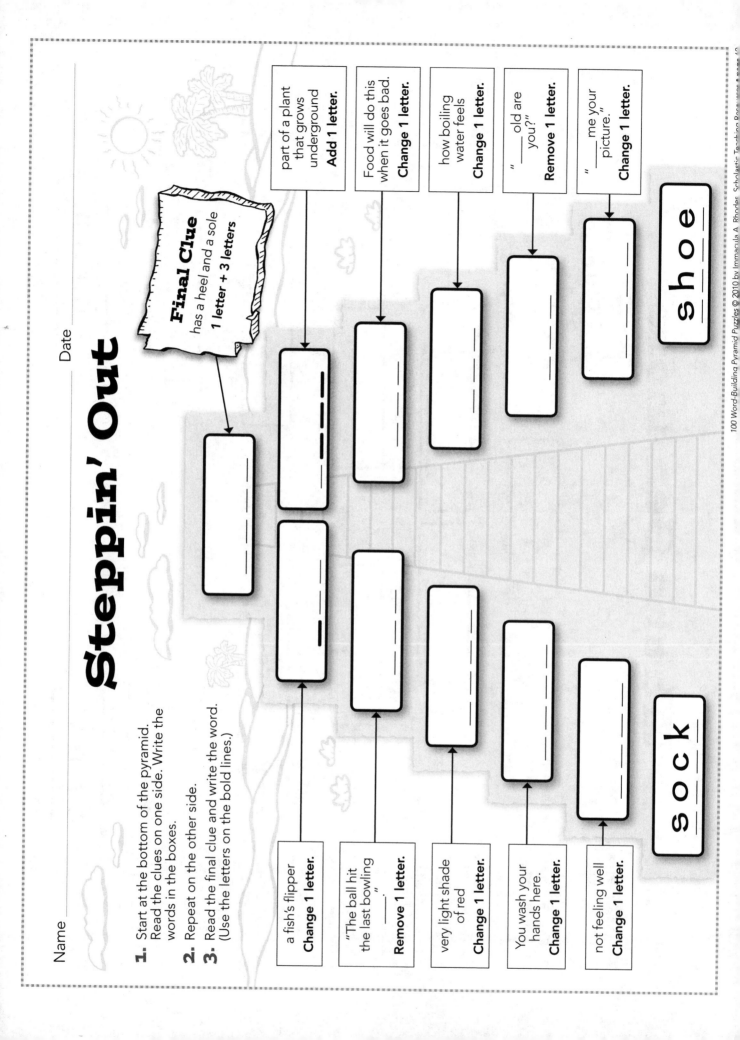

part of a plant that grows underground
Add 1 letter.

Food will do this when it goes bad.
Change 1 letter.

how boiling water feels
Change 1 letter.

"_____ old are you?"
Remove 1 letter.

"_____ me your picture."
Change 1 letter.

s h o e

a fish's flipper
Change 1 letter.

"The ball hit the last bowling _____."
Remove 1 letter.

very light shade of red
Change 1 letter.

You wash your hands here.
Change 1 letter.

not feeling well
Change 1 letter.

s o c k

Name _____ Date _____

1. Start at the bottom of the pyramid. Read the clues on one side. Write the words in the boxes.
2. Repeat on the other side.
3. Read the final clue and write the word. (Use the letters on the bold lines.)

Final Clue
to figure out something
"Did you ___ the answer?"
1 letter + 3 letters

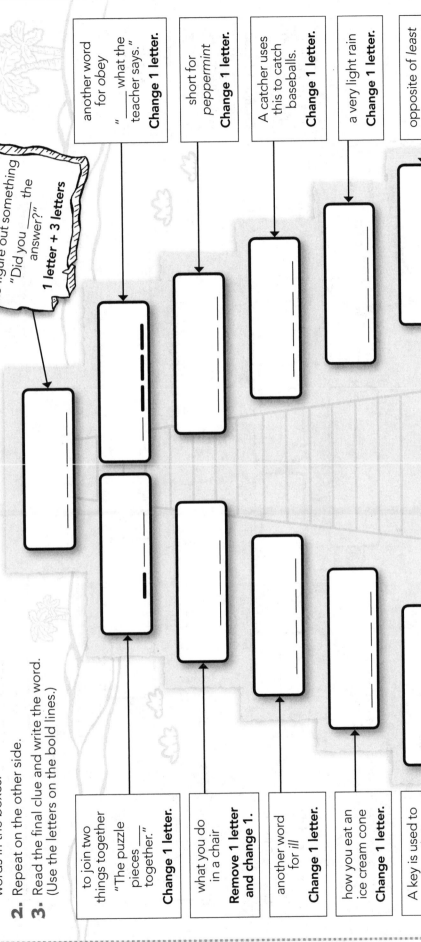

another word for obey
"___ what the teacher says."
Change 1 letter.

short for *peppermint*
Change 1 letter.

A catcher uses this to catch baseballs.
Change 1 letter.

a very light rain
Change 1 letter.

opposite of *least*
Change 1 letter.

l o s t

to join two things together
"The puzzle pieces ___ together."
Change 1 letter.

what you do in a chair
Remove 1 letter and change 1.

another word for *ill*
Change 1 letter.

how you eat an ice cream cone
Change 1 letter.

A key is used to open this.
Change 1 letter.

l o o k

Date _____

Freshwater Friends

1. Start at the bottom of the pyramid. Read the clues on one side. Write the words in the boxes.
2. Repeat on the other side.
3. Read the final clue and write the word. (Use the letters on the bold lines.)

Final Clue
a small body of water
1 letter + 3 letters

Clues (one side):

like very much
"I'm ____ of soft kittens."
Change 1 letter.

opposite of lose
Add 1 letter.

A whale uses its tail ____ to swim.
Change 1 letter.

the right size
"My shoes ____ my feet well."
Remove 1 letter.

A boxer punches with this.
Change 1 letter.

Clues (other side):

"I get to feed the class ____ today."
Change 1 letter.

to allow
Change 1 letter.

Your foot is attached to this.
Change 1 letter.

a long, round piece of wood
Change 1 letter.

a thick cloud near the ground
Remove 1 letter.

f i s h

f r o g

Name ______________________ Date ______________

Moving Along

1. Start at the bottom of the pyramid. Read the clues on one side. Write the words in the boxes.
2. Repeat on the other side.
3. Read the final clue and write the word. (Use the letters on the bold lines.)

Final Clue
animal that hisses and has no legs
2 letters + 3 letters

_ _ _ _ _

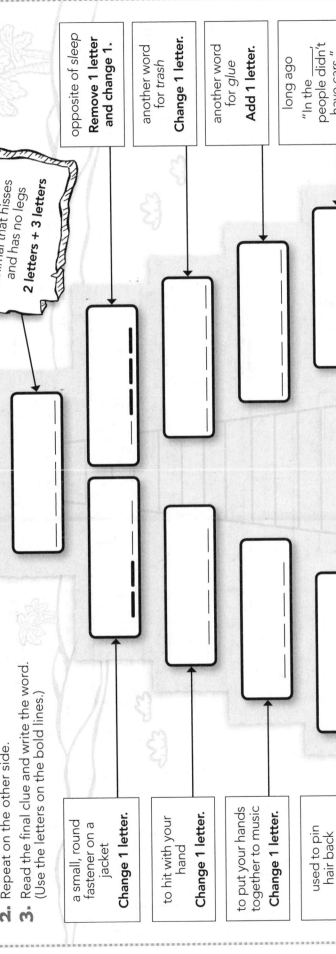

Left side clue	Left word	Right word	Right side clue
a small, round fastener on a jacket **Change 1 letter.**	**_ _** _ _	_ **_ _ _**	opposite of *sleep* **Remove 1 letter and change 1.**
to hit with your hand **Change 1 letter.**	_ _ _ _	_ _ _ _ _	another word for *trash* **Change 1 letter.**
to put your hands together to music **Change 1 letter.**	_ _ _ _	_ _ _ _ _	another word for *glue* **Add 1 letter.**
used to pin hair back **Change 1 letter.**	_ _ _ _	_ _ _ _	long ago "In the ____, people didn't have cars." **Change 1 letter.**
to fall on something wet **Remove 1 letter and change 1.**	_ _ _ _	_ _ _ _	opposite of *fail* **Remove 1 letter and change 1.**
	s l i d e	g r a s s	

Name _____

Date _____

Are You Thirsty?

1. Start at the bottom of the pyramid. Read the clues on one side. Write the words in the boxes.
2. Repeat on the other side.
3. Read the final clue and write the word. (Use the letters on the bold lines.)

Final Clue
You do this with milk or juice.
2 letters + 3 letters

_____ [box]

a pale red color
Add 1 letter.

_____ [box]

another word for tack
Change 1 letter.

_____ [box]

a deep hole
Change 1 letter.

_____ [box]

to set something down
"_____ the box over there."
Change 1 letter.

_____ [box]

opposite of in
Remove 2 letters.

_____ [box]

m o u t h

to pull something along the ground
Add 1 letter.

_____ [box]

an old cloth used for cleaning
Change 1 letter.

_____ [box]

another word for *label*
Change 1 letter.

_____ [box]

a light touch with your finger
Change 1 letter.

_____ [box]

another word for *lid*
Change 1 letter.

_____ [box]

c u p

Name

Date

It's Wintertime!

1. Start at the bottom of the pyramid. Read the clues on one side. Write the words in the boxes.
2. Repeat on the other side.
3. Read the final clue and write the word. (Use the letters on the bold lines.)

Final Clue
white flakes that fall from the sky
2 letters + 2 letters

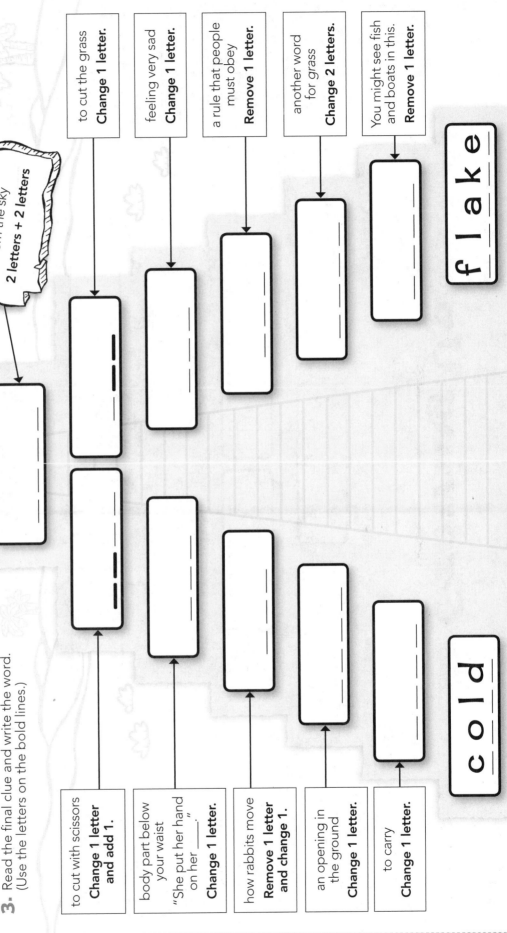

to cut the grass **Change 1 letter.**

feeling very sad **Change 1 letter.**

a rule that people must obey **Remove 1 letter.**

another word for *grass* **Change 2 letters.**

You might see fish and boats in this. **Remove 1 letter.**

to cut with scissors **Change 1 letter and add 1.**

body part below your waist "She put her hand on her ____." **Change 1 letter.**

how rabbits move **Remove 1 letter and change 1.**

an opening in the ground **Change 1 letter.**

to carry **Change 1 letter.**

f l a k e

c o l d

Name _____

Date _____

Growing Up

1. Start at the bottom of the pyramid. Read the clues on one side. Write the words in the boxes.

2. Repeat on the other side.

3. Read the final clue and write the word. (Use the letters on the bold lines.)

Final Clue
to bury a seed in soil
2 letters + 3 letters

to breathe hard
Add 1 letter.

a skillet
Change 1 letter.

to tap someone lightly on the head
Change 1 letter.

Coffee can be made in this.
Change 1 letter.

An old log does this.
Remove 1 letter.

r o o t

sound of something dropping into water
Add 1 letter.

another word for dad
Change 1 letter.

a lid
Remove 1 letter.

to put an end to
Change 1 letter.

another word for stair
Change 1 letter.

s t e m

Name ______________________ Date ______________

At School

1. Start at the bottom of the pyramid. Read the clues on one side. Write the words in the boxes.
2. Repeat on the other side.
3. Read the final clue and write the word. (Use the letters on the bold lines.)

Final Clue
to help students learn
1 letter + 4 letters

_ _ _ _ _

Left side clues	Left side boxes	Right side boxes	Right side clues
black coating that covers a road **Change 1 letter.**	_ _ _	_ _ _ _ _	a fuzzy fruit that has a pit **Add 1 letter.**
a tall counter "We sat on tall stools at the breakfast ___." **Change 1 letter.**	_ _ _	_ _ _ _	every one **Change 1 letter and add 1.**
opposite of *good* **Remove 1 letter.**	_ _ _	_ _ _	what you do at a meal **Change 1 letter.**
"A ___ fell off of my necklace." **Change 1 letter.**	_ _ _ _	_ _ _	"My dad gave me a ___ on the back." **Remove 1 letter and change 1.**
to show the way **Remove 1 letter and change 1.**	_ _ _ _	_ _ _ _	to end "I hope the storm will ___ soon." **Remove 1 letter and change 1.**
	learn	class	

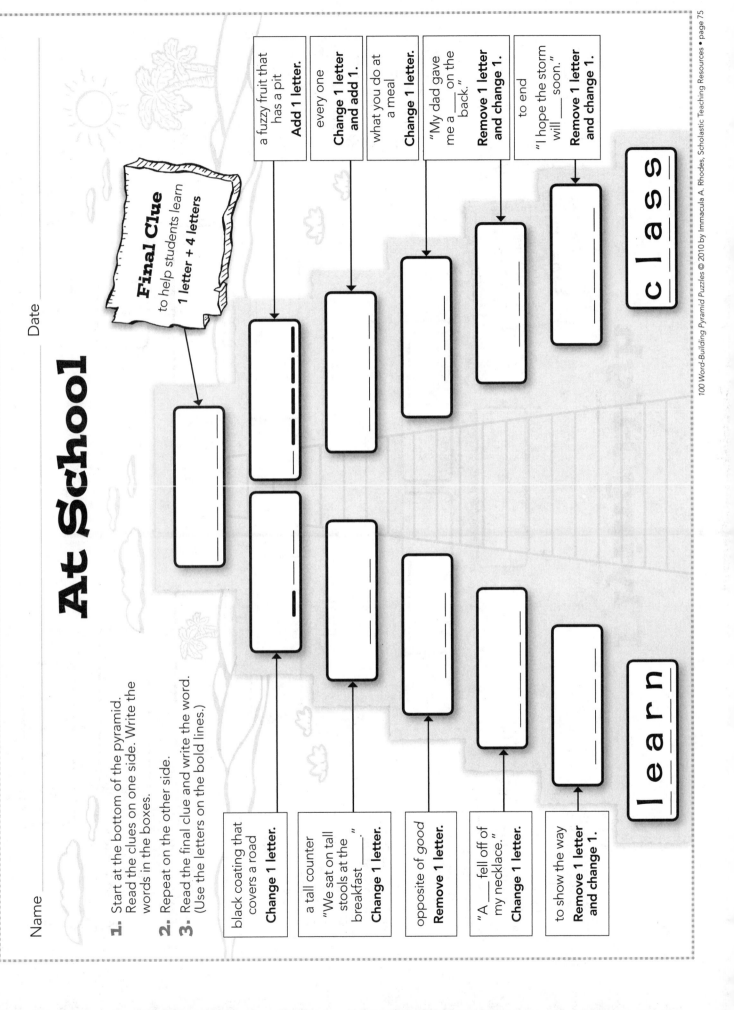

Name _____

Date _____

Flying High

1. Start at the bottom of the pyramid. Read the clues on one side. Write the words in the boxes.
2. Repeat on the other side.
3. Read the final clue and write the word. (Use the letters on the bold lines.)

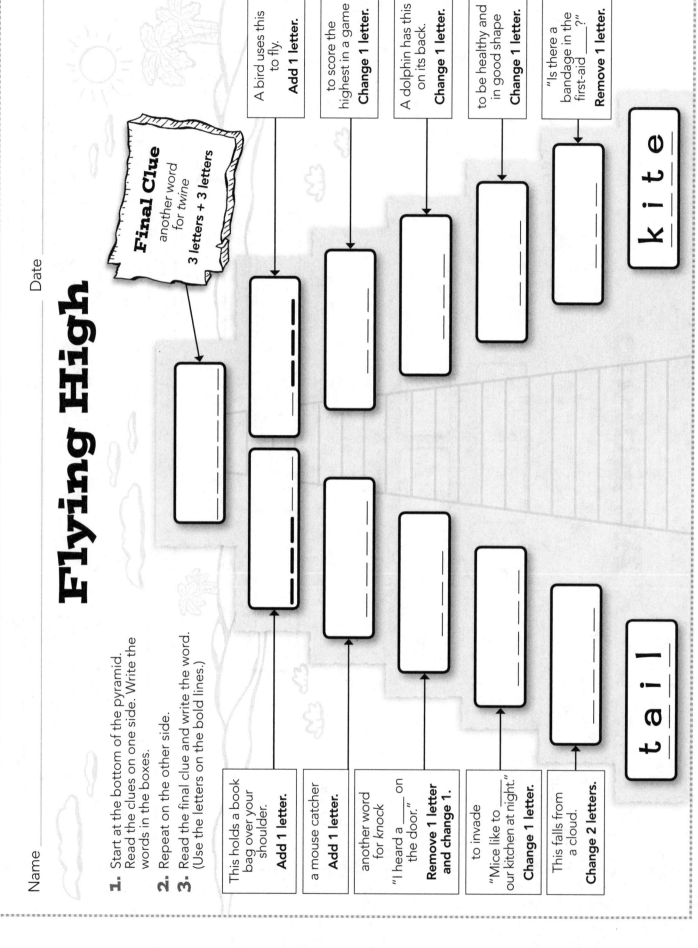

Final Clue
another word for twine
3 letters + 3 letters

A bird uses this to fly.
Add 1 letter.

to score the highest in a game
Change 1 letter.

A dolphin has this on its back.
Change 1 letter.

to be healthy and in good shape
Change 1 letter.

"Is there a bandage in the first-aid _____?"
Remove 1 letter.

k i t e

This holds a book bag over your shoulder.
Add 1 letter.

a mouse catcher
Add 1 letter.

another word for knock
"I heard a _____ on the door."
Remove 1 letter and change 1.

to invade
"Mice like to our kitchen at night."
Change 1 letter.

This falls from a cloud.
Change 2 letters.

t a i l

Name _____   Date _____

Sip It Up

1. Start at the bottom of the pyramid. Read the clues on one side. Write the words in the boxes.
2. Repeat on the other side.
3. Read the final clue and write the word. (Use the letters on the bold lines.)

Final Clue
You sip a drink through this.
3 letters + 2 letters

A crab pinches with this. **Add 1 letter.**

People who break this may go to jail. **Change 1 letter.**

short word for laboratory **Change 1 letter.**

"Dad held the baby on his ___." **Change 1 letter.**

a kind of hat **Change 1 letter.**

c u p

to wander off **Add 1 letter.**

Use this to carry food on. **Change 1 letter and add 1.**

dried grasses that horses eat **Change 1 letter.**

"Jim ___ to go home early." **Change 1 letter.**

past tense of *hide* **Change 1 letter.**

l i d

Name _____   Date _____

In the Cafeteria

1. Start at the bottom of the pyramid. Read the clues on one side. Write the words in the boxes.
2. Repeat on the other side.
3. Read the final clue and write the word. (Use the letters on the bold lines.)

Final Clue
You sit down at a table to eat this.
1 letter + 3 letters

not fake
Change 1 letter.

to close an envelope
Change 1 letter.

"I'll sit in the back of the car."
_____ **Change 1 letter.**

Your heart does this in your chest.
Change 1 letter.

another word for *tidy*
Add 1 letter.

e a t

opposite of *woman*
Change 1 letter.

someone who loves a sport, like baseball
Change 1 letter.

Something you enjoy doing is ___.
Change 1 letter.

A hot dog is put in this.
Remove 2 letters.

a cluster of grapes
Change 1 letter.

l u n c h

Name _____

Date _____

Good for You

1. Start at the bottom of the pyramid. Read the clues on one side. Write the words in the boxes.
2. Repeat on the other side.
3. Read the final clue and write the word. (Use the letters on the bold lines.)

Final Clue
a special food, gift, or surprise
2 letters + 3 letters

Clues (left side, top to bottom)

to make something hot
Add 1 letter.

You do this to an apple or pear.
Change 1 letter.

past tense of sit
Remove 1 letter and change 1.

Things you buy are put in this.
Remove 1 letter.

to put one thing on top of another
Change 1 letter.

s n a c k

Clues (right side, bottom to top)

a long ride
Add 1 letter.

to tear something in two
Change 1 letter.

to take a small drink of milk
Change 1 letter.

"_____ on the floor and cross your legs."
Remove 1 letter.

a pair of pants and jacket that match
Remove 1 letter and change 1.

f r u i t

Name _____

Date _____

Baby Bird

1. Start at the bottom of the pyramid. Read the clues on one side. Write the words in the boxes.
2. Repeat on the other side.
3. Read the final clue and write the word. (Use the letters on the bold lines.)

Final Clue
to travel through the air
2 letters + 1 letter

to do the best you can
Remove 1 letter and change 1.

to stumble or fall
Add 1 letter.

to tear something
Change 1 letter.

You push this out when you pout.
Change 1 letter.

"Put your hands in your ____."
Remove 1 letter.

f l a p

smooth and even
"The top of the table is ____."
Add 1 letter.

opposite of *thin*
Change 1 letter.

"Can you ____ this book in your bag?"
Change 1 letter.

part of a fish
Change 1 letter.

to get the top prize
Remove 1 letter.

w i n g

Name _____

Date _____

Pump and Pedal

1. Start at the bottom of the pyramid. Read the clues on one side. Write the words in the boxes.

2. Repeat on the other side.

3. Read the final clue and write the word. (Use the letters on the bold lines.)

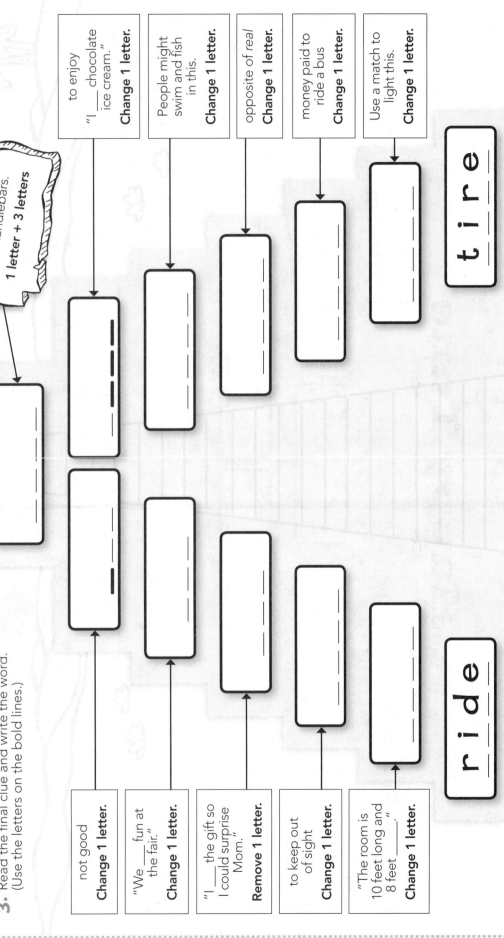

Final Clue
This has two wheels and handlebars.
1 letter + 3 letters

to enjoy
"I ____ chocolate ice cream."
Change 1 letter.

People might swim and fish in this.
Change 1 letter.

opposite of *real*
Change 1 letter.

money paid to ride a bus
Change 1 letter.

Use a match to light this.
Change 1 letter.

not good
Change 1 letter.

"We ____ fun at the fair."
Change 1 letter.

"I ____ the gift so I could surprise Mom."
Remove 1 letter.

to keep out of sight
Change 1 letter.

"The room is 10 feet long and 8 feet ____."
Change 1 letter.

t i r e

r i d e

Name _____

Date _____

Happy Tune

1. Start at the bottom of the pyramid. Read the clues on one side. Write the words in the boxes.
2. Repeat on the other side.
3. Read the final clue and write the word. (Use the letters on the bold lines.)

Final Clue
words that are set to music
1 letter + 3 letters

opposite of short
Change 1 letter.

only one person or thing
Change 1 letter.

one part of a skeleton
Change 2 letters.

a wild pig
Change 1 letter.

a large, furry animal that has cubs
Change 1 letter.

b e a t

"Goldilocks ____ in the little chair."
Change 1 letter.

not skinny
Change 1 letter.

a long distance away
Change 1 letter.

This is pulled by a train engine.
Change 1 letter.

a lid for a bottle
Remove 1 letter.

c l a p

Name _____   Date _____

Taking a Drive

1. Start at the bottom of the pyramid. Read the clues on one side. Write the words in the boxes.
2. Repeat on the other side.
3. Read the final clue and write the word. (Use the letters on the bold lines.)

Final Clue
another word for street
1 letter + 3 letters

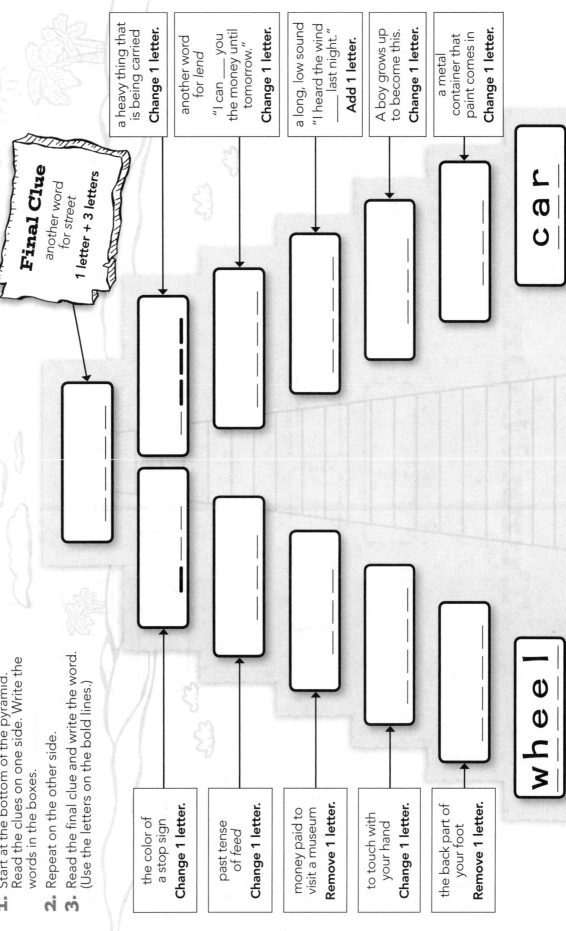

Right-side clues (top):
- a heavy thing that is being carried **Change 1 letter.**
- another word for lend "I can ____ you the money until tomorrow." **Change 1 letter.**
- a long, low sound "I heard the wind ____ last night." **Add 1 letter.**
- A boy grows up to become this. **Change 1 letter.**
- a metal container that paint comes in **Change 1 letter.**

Bottom clues (left side):
- the color of a stop sign **Change 1 letter.**
- past tense of *feed* **Change 1 letter.**
- money paid to visit a museum **Remove 1 letter.**
- to touch with your hand **Change 1 letter.**
- the back part of your foot **Remove 1 letter.**

c a r

w h e e l

w r

Name _____

Date _____

Turn It On

1. Start at the bottom of the pyramid. Read the clues on one side. Write the words in the boxes.
2. Repeat on the other side.
3. Read the final clue and write the word. (Use the letters on the bold lines.)

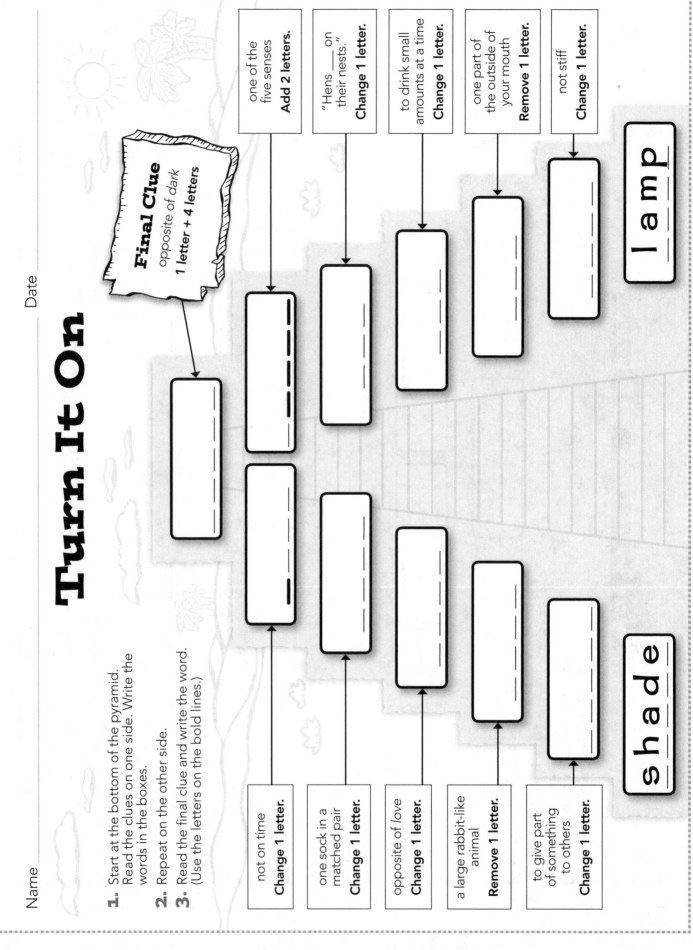

Final Clue
opposite of dark
1 letter + 4 letters

one of the five senses
Add 2 letters.

"Hens ___ on their nests."
Change 1 letter.

to drink small amounts at a time
Change 1 letter.

one part of the outside of your mouth
Remove 1 letter.

not stiff
Change 1 letter.

l a m p

not on time
Change 1 letter.

one sock in a matched pair
Change 1 letter.

opposite of love
Change 1 letter.

a large rabbit-like animal
Remove 1 letter.

to give part of something to others
Change 1 letter.

s h a d e

Name _____

Date _____

Time to Eat!

1. Start at the bottom of the pyramid. Read the clues on one side. Write the words in the boxes.
2. Repeat on the other side.
3. Read the final clue and write the word. (Use the letters on the bold lines.)

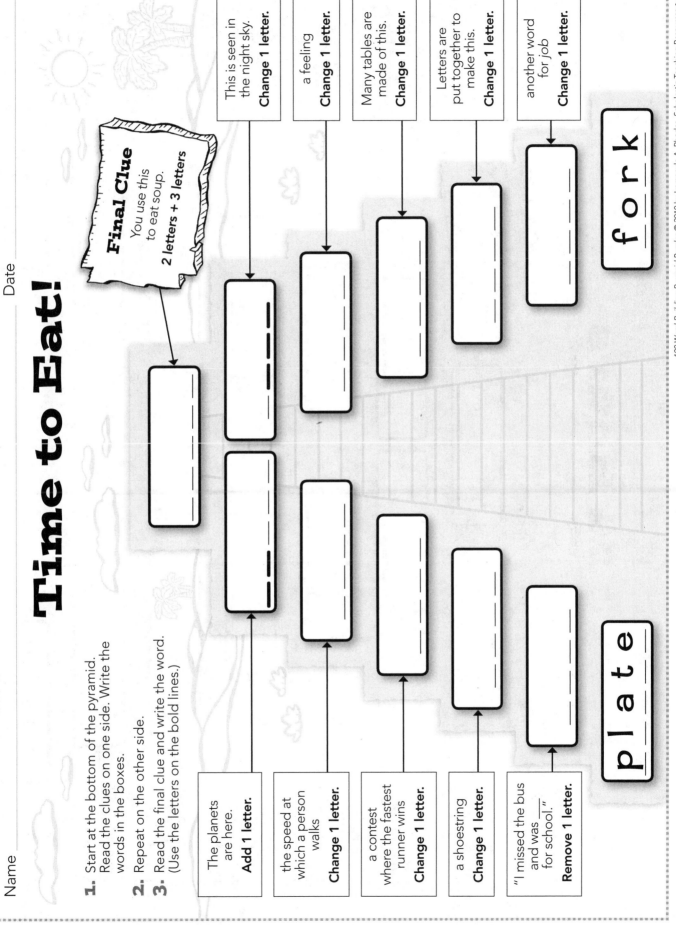

Final Clue
You use this to eat soup.
2 letters + 3 letters

This is seen in the night sky.
Change 1 letter.

a feeling
Change 1 letter.

Many tables are made of this.
Change 1 letter.

Letters are put together to make this.
Change 1 letter.

another word for job
Change 1 letter.

f o r k

The planets are here.
Add 1 letter.

the speed at which a person walks
Change 1 letter.

a contest where the fastest runner wins
Change 1 letter.

a shoestring
Change 1 letter.

"I missed the bus and was _____ for school."
Remove 1 letter.

p l a t e

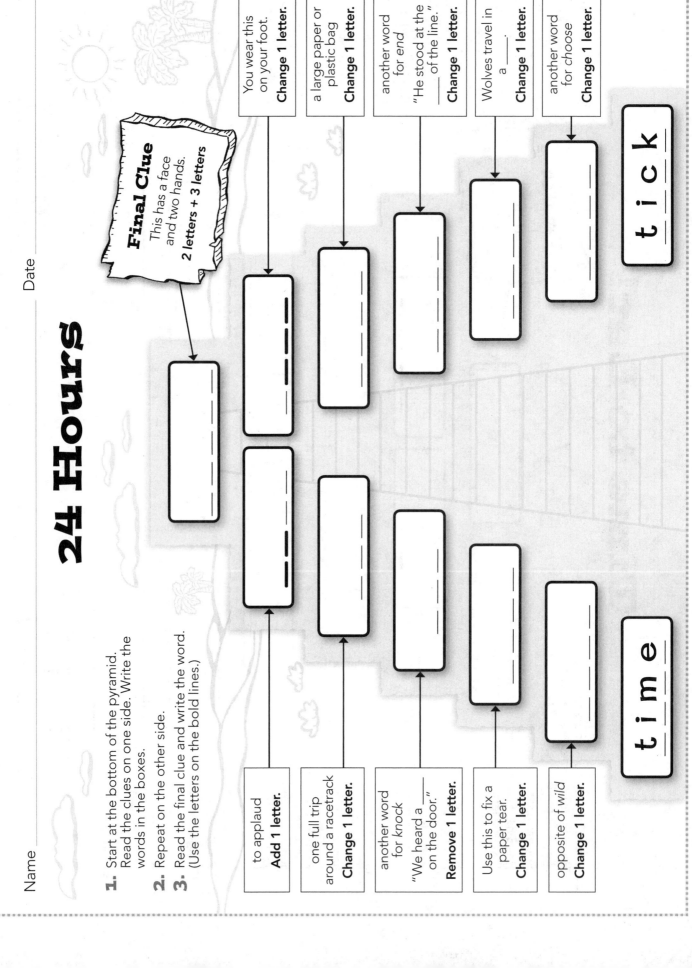

24 Hours

Name _____   Date _____

1. Start at the bottom of the pyramid. Read the clues on one side. Write the words in the boxes.
2. Repeat on the other side.
3. Read the final clue and write the word. (Use the letters on the bold lines.)

Final Clue
This has a face and two hands.
2 letters + 3 letters

You wear this on your foot. **Change 1 letter.**

a large paper or plastic bag **Change 1 letter.**

another word for *end*
"He stood at the ____ of the line." **Change 1 letter.**

Wolves travel in a ____. **Change 1 letter.**

another word for *choose* **Change 1 letter.**

to applaud **Add 1 letter.**

one full trip around a racetrack **Change 1 letter.**

another word for *knock*
"We heard a ____ on the door." **Remove 1 letter.**

Use this to fix a paper tear. **Change 1 letter.**

opposite of *wild* **Change 1 letter.**

t i c k

t i m e

Name _____

Date _____

In the Dark Sky

1. Start at the bottom of the pyramid. Read the clues on one side. Write the words in the boxes.
2. Repeat on the other side.
3. Read the final clue and write the word. (Use the letters on the bold lines.)

Final Clue
opposite of day
1 letter + 4 letters

to argue with someone
Add 2 letters.

a small, dark fruit with lots of seeds
Change 1 letter.

what you do with a shovel
Change 1 letter.

another word for large
Change 1 letter.

past tense of *bite*
Change 1 letter.

b a t

close by
Change 1 letter.

a fruit shaped like a light bulb
Add 1 letter.

This tiny green vegetable grows in a pod.
Change 1 letter.

a drink that can be served hot or cold
Change 1 letter.

a jumping insect found on animals
Remove 1 letter and change 1.

Change 1 letter and add 1.

f l y

Name _____

Date _____

Waddling Along

1. Start at the bottom of the pyramid. Read the clues on one side. Write the words in the boxes.
2. Repeat on the other side.
3. Read the final clue and write the word. (Use the letters on the bold lines.)

Final Clue
a water bird with short legs and webbed feet
1 letter + 3 letters

good fortune
Change 1 letter.

"____ your car door to be safe."
Change 1 letter.

to move from side to side
"Mom will ____ the baby to sleep."
Change 1 letter.

Clothes are hung on this in a store.
Change 1 letter.

a small nail
Remove 1 letter and change 1.

q u a c k

to eat
Change 1 letter.

Stand one behind another in this.
"Let's ____ up for lunch."
Change 1 letter.

a pit where coal is found
Change 1 letter.

the part of you that thinks
"Please make up your ____."
Change 1 letter.

to hold together
"Let's ____ the pages of the book together."
Change 1 letter.

b i r d

Name _____

Date _____

On a Lily Pad

1. Start at the bottom of the pyramid. Read the clues on one side. Write the words in the boxes.
2. Repeat on the other side.
3. Read the final clue and write the word. (Use the letters on the bold lines.)

Final Clue
a pond animal that looks like a toad
2 letter + 2 letters

Clues (right side):

a pet that barks
Change 1 letter.

the top of an *i*
Change 1 letter.

very much
"I like ice cream a ____."
Change 1 letter.

a small bed used for camping
Change 1 letter.

a police officer
Change 1 letter.

hop

Clues (left side):

to cook something in oil
Change 1 letter.

Birds flap their wings to do this.
Change 1 letter.

sneaky
Remove 1 letter and change 1.

another word for hit
Add 1 letter.

to drink with the tongue
"Spot likes to ____ up water from puddles."
Remove 1 letter.

leap

Outer Space

Name _____ Date _____

1. Start at the bottom of the pyramid. Read the clues on one side. Write the words in the boxes.
2. Repeat on the other side.
3. Read the final clue and write the word. (Use the letters on the bold lines.)

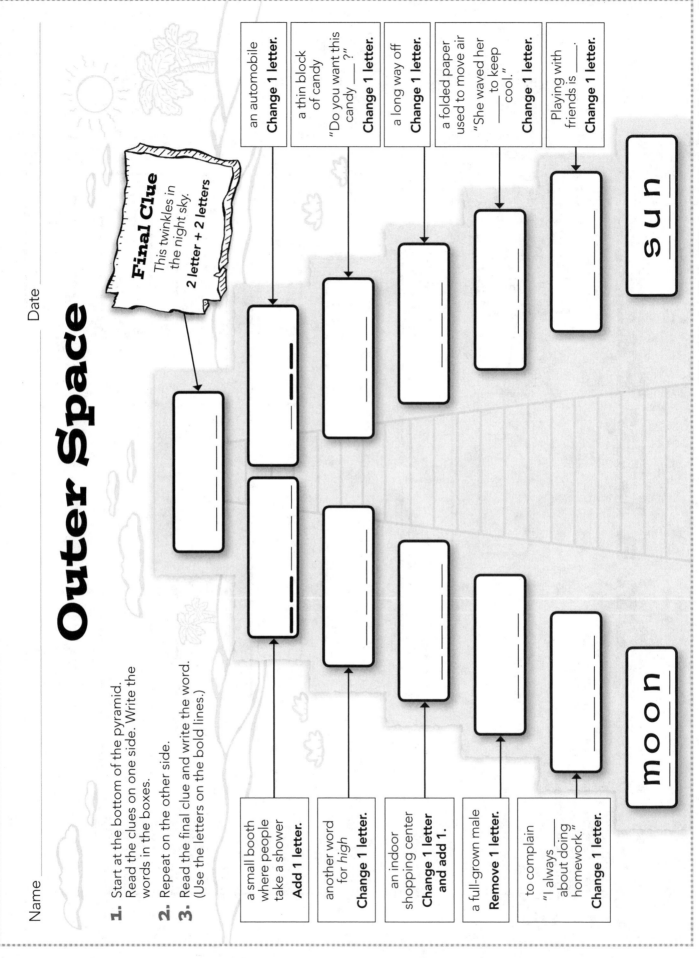

Final Clue

This twinkles in the night sky.

2 letter + 2 letters

Right-side clues:

- an automobile **Change 1 letter.**
- a thin block of candy "Do you want this candy ____?" **Change 1 letter.**
- a long way off **Change 1 letter.**
- a folded paper used to move air "She waved her ____ to keep cool." **Change 1 letter.**
- Playing with friends is ____. **Change 1 letter.**

s u n

Left-side clues:

- a small booth where people take a shower **Add 1 letter.**
- another word for *high* **Change 1 letter.**
- an indoor shopping center **Change 1 letter and add 1.**
- a full-grown male **Remove 1 letter.**
- to complain "I always ____ about doing homework." **Change 1 letter.**

m o o n

Name _____

Date _____

Feathery Swimmer

1. Start at the bottom of the pyramid. Read the clues on one side. Write the words in the boxes.

2. Repeat on the other side.

3. Read the final clue and write the word. (Use the letters on the bold lines.)

Final Clue
the sound a duck makes
2 letters + 3 letters

You sit on this part of a horse.
Change 1 letter and add 1.

to hit at something
"I tried to ____ the bee away."
Change 1 letter.

"I ____ I'm taller than you."
Remove 1 letter.

a strap used to hold up pants
Change 1 letter.

a metal object that rings
Change 1 letter.

b i l l

to give up
Change 1 letter and add 1.

"This size is a perfect ____."
Change 1 letter.

past tense of *light*
The fireworks ____ up the sky.
Remove 1 letter and change 1.

how you eat a lollipop
Change 1 letter.

"Good ____ on your test."
Change 1 letter.

d u c k

Name _____

Date _____

In the Ground

1. Start at the bottom of the pyramid. Read the clues on one side. Write the words in the boxes.
2. Repeat on the other side.
3. Read the final clue and write the word. (Use the letters on the bold lines.)

Final Clue
another word for dirt
1 letter + 3 letters

to heat water until it bubbles
Change 1 letter.

to scoop water out of a boat
Change 1 letter.

This is hit or thrown in a game.
Change 1 letter.

"I have a dollar ____ to spend."
Change 1 letter and add 1.

something that is great in size
Change 1 letter.

d i g

when stores sell things at lower prices
"Is that hat on ____?"
Change 1 letter.

opposite of *female*
Change 1 letter.

a freckle-like bump
Change 1 letter.

opposite of *less*
Change 1 letter.

past tense of *wear*
Change 1 letter.

w o r m

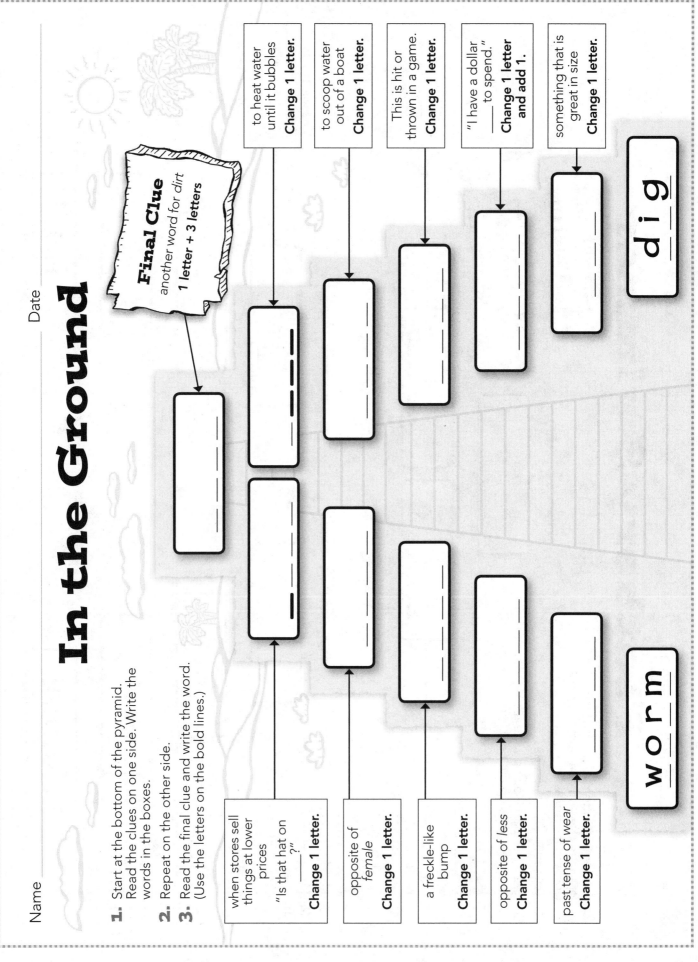

Name _____

Date _____

Around the Barn

1. Start at the bottom of the pyramid. Read the clues on one side. Write the words in the boxes.
2. Repeat on the other side.
3. Read the final clue and write the word. (Use the letters on the bold lines.)

Final Clue
a place where animals are raised

1 letter + 3 letters

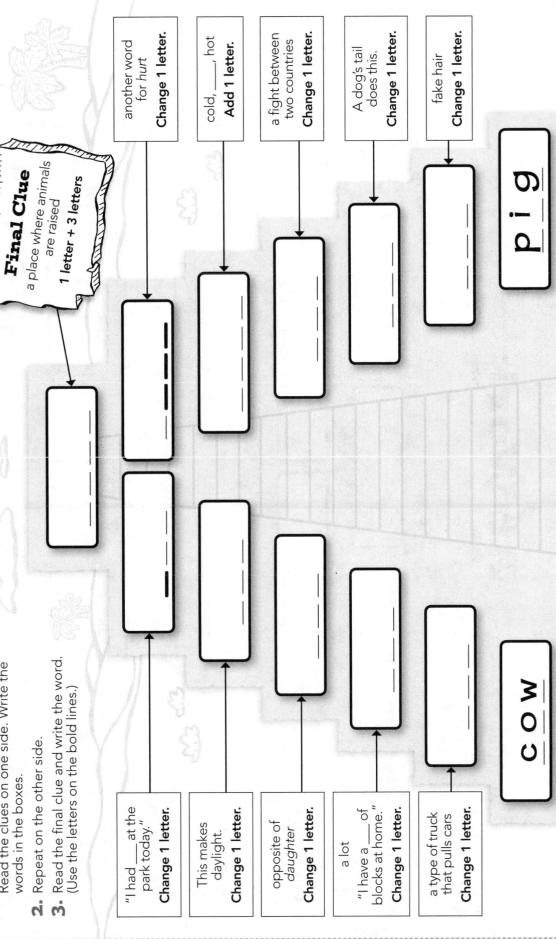

another word for *hurt*
Change 1 letter.

cold, ____, hot
Add 1 letter.

a fight between two countries
Change 1 letter.

A dog's tail does this.
Change 1 letter.

fake hair
Change 1 letter.

p i g

"I had ____ at the park today."
Change 1 letter.

This makes daylight.
Change 1 letter.

opposite of *daughter*
Change 1 letter.

a lot
"I have a ____ of blocks at home."
Change 1 letter.

a type of truck that pulls cars
Change 1 letter.

c o w

Name ______________________ Date ______________

At Work

1. Start at the bottom of the pyramid. Read the clues on one side. Write the words in the boxes.
2. Repeat on the other side.
3. Read the final clue and write the word. (Use the letters on the bold lines.)

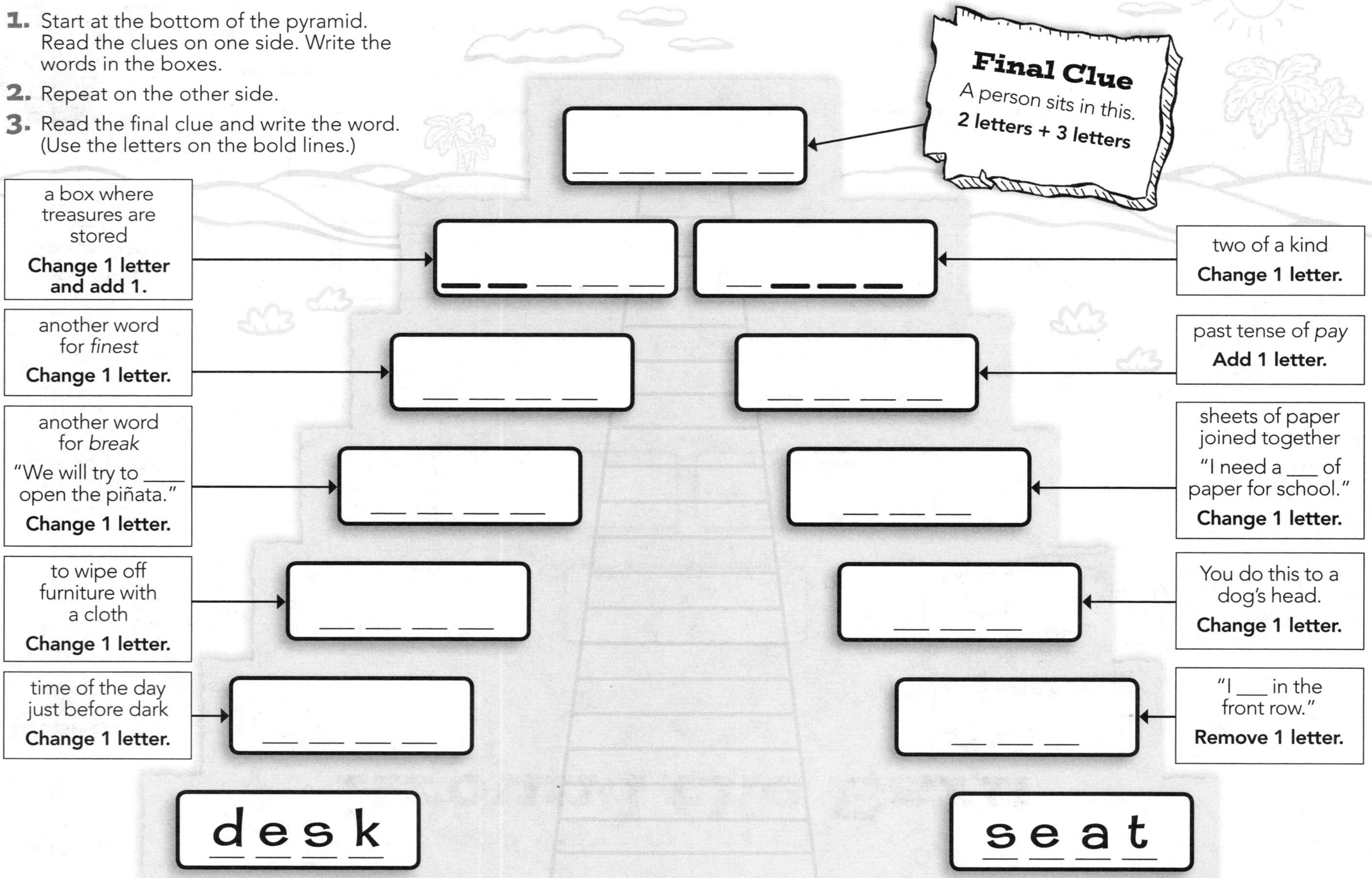

Final Clue
A person sits in this.
2 letters + 3 letters
a box where treasures are stored
Change 1 letter and add 1.
another word for *finest*
Change 1 letter.
another word for *break*
"We will try to ____ open the piñata."
Change 1 letter.
to wipe off furniture with a cloth
Change 1 letter.
time of the day just before dark
Change 1 letter.
desk
two of a kind
Change 1 letter.
past tense of *pay*
Add 1 letter.
sheets of paper joined together
"I need a ___ of paper for school."
Change 1 letter.
You do this to a dog's head.
Change 1 letter.
"I ___ in the front row."
Remove 1 letter.
seat

Name _____

Date _____

Up on Top

1. Start at the bottom of the pyramid. Read the clues on one side. Write the words in the boxes.

2. Repeat on the other side.

3. Read the final clue and write the word. (Use the letters on the bold lines.)

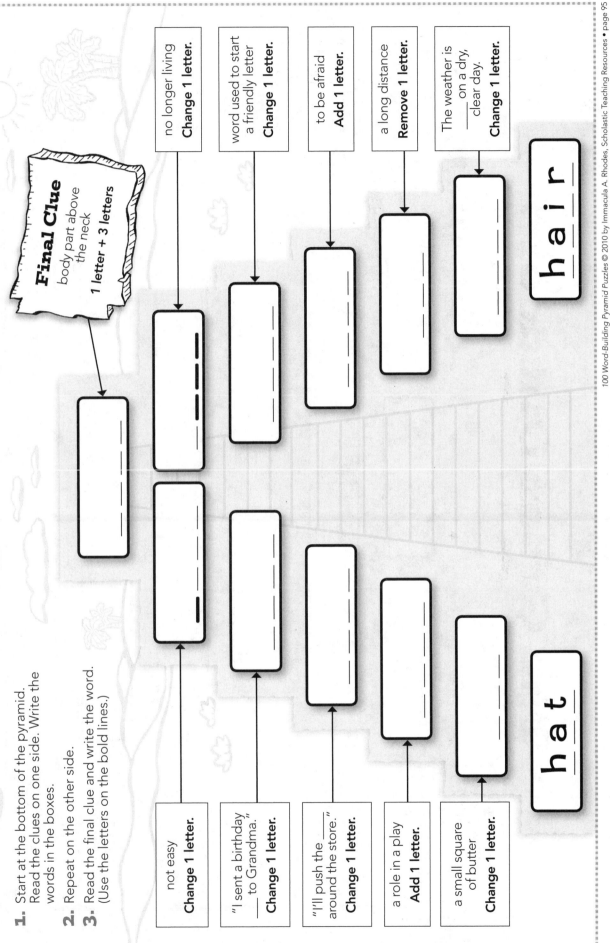

Final Clue
body part above the neck
1 letter + 3 letters

no longer living
Change 1 letter.

word used to start a friendly letter
Change 1 letter.

to be afraid
Add 1 letter.

a long distance
Remove 1 letter.

The weather is ___ on a dry, clear day.
Change 1 letter.

h a i r

not easy
Change 1 letter.

"I sent a birthday ___ to Grandma."
Change 1 letter.

"I'll push the ___ around the store."
Change 1 letter.

a role in a play
Add 1 letter.

a small square of butter
Change 1 letter.

h a t

The Great Outdoors

Name _____   Date _____

1. Start at the bottom of the pyramid. Read the clues on one side. Write the words in the boxes.
2. Repeat on the other side.
3. Read the final clue and write the word. (Use the letters on the bold lines.)

Final Clue
another word for ocean
1 letter + 2 letters

This grows in a pod on a vine. **Change 1 letter.**

a cat or dog that lives with people **Change 1 letter.**

to touch quickly with a flat hand **Change 1 letter.**

Nan ____ in the chair next to me. **Change 1 letter.**

to speak something **Change 1 letter.**

s k y

"Let's ____ on the park bench." **Change 1 letter.**

another word for *punch* **Change 1 letter.**

Wear this to keep your head warm. **Change 1 letter.**

past tense of *has* **Remove 1 letter.**

This has a palm and fingers. **Change 1 letter.**

l a n d

Name _____

Date _____

On the Map

1. Start at the bottom of the pyramid. Read the clues on one side. Write the words in the boxes.
2. Repeat on the other side.
3. Read the final clue and write the word. (Use the letters on the bold lines.)

Final Clue
one of 50 in the USA
2 letters + 3 letters

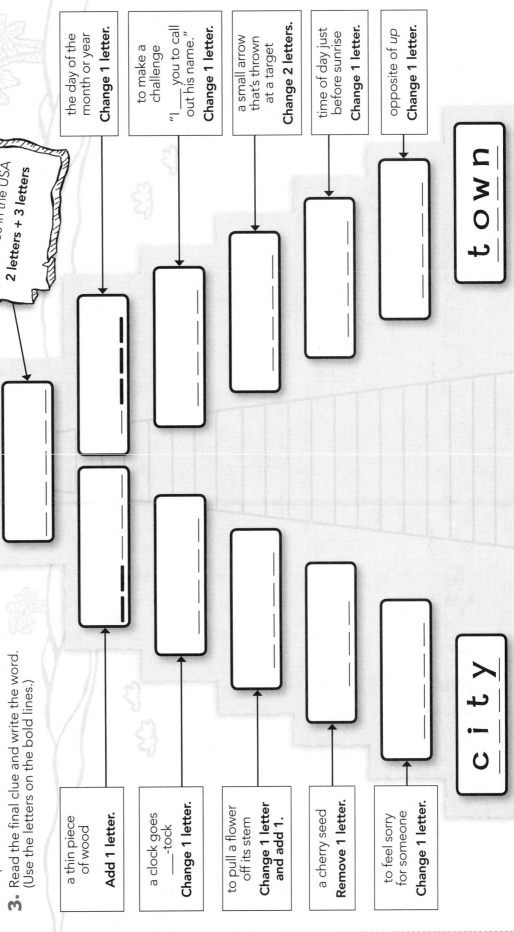

the day of the month or year
Change 1 letter.

to make a challenge "I ___ you to call out his name."
Change 1 letter.

a small arrow that's thrown at a target
Change 2 letters.

time of day just before sunrise
Change 1 letter.

opposite of up
Change 1 letter.

t o w n

a thin piece of wood
Add 1 letter.

a clock goes ___ -tock
Change 1 letter.

to pull a flower off its stem
Change 1 letter and add 1.

a cherry seed
Remove 1 letter.

to feel sorry for someone
Change 1 letter.

c i t y

Name _____

Date _____

Twinkle, Twinkle

1. Start at the bottom of the pyramid.
   Read the clues on one side. Write the
   words in the boxes.

2. Repeat on the other side.

3. Read the final clue and write the word.
   (Use the letters on the bold lines.)

Final Clue

giving out a lot of light

2 letters + 4 letters

a battle
Add 2 letters.

a soft, dark,
pear-shaped fruit
Change 1 letter.

"Mr. Chavez
exercises
to stay ____."
Change 1 letter.

This helps
a fish swim.
Remove 1 letter.

good or great
"You did a ____
job on your
painting."
**Remove 1 letter
and change 1.**

s h i n e

"May I ____ my
new book to
school?"
Add 1 letter.

Wear this on
your finger.
Change 1 letter.

to make music
with your voice
**Change 1 letter
and add 1.**

a polite way to
address a man
Remove 1 letter.

to mix together
with a spoon
Change 1 letter.

s t a r

Warm and Toasty

1. Start at the bottom of the pyramid. Read the clues on one side. Write the words in the boxes.
2. Repeat on the other side.
3. Read the final clue and write the word. (Use the letters on the bold lines.)

Final Clue
This comes from trees.
1 letter + 3 letters

a feeling "I am in a great _____ today!"
Change 1 letter.

This orbits around the Earth.
Change 1 letter.

not long from now
Change 1 letter and add 1.

The planets orbit around this.
Change 1 letter.

bread that a hamburger is put on
Remove 1 letter.

"_____ you waiting for me?"
Change 1 letter.

in this place
Change 1 letter.

to give someone a job
Change 1 letter.

a wheel
Change 1 letter.

a very thin electrical cord
Change 1 letter.

b u r n

f i r e

Name _____

Date _____

Saddle Up!

1. Start at the bottom of the pyramid. Read the clues on one side. Write the words in the boxes.
2. Repeat on the other side.
3. Read the final clue and write the word. (Use the letters on the bold lines.)

Final Clue
to travel on a horse's back
1 letter + 3 letters

the rise and fall of the sea
Change 1 letter.

the hour and minutes on a clock
Add 1 letter.

when teams have the same score
Change 1 letter.

Each of your feet has one big ____.
Change 1 letter.

a garden tool
Remove 2 letters.

This covers the floor.
Change 1 letter.

to wrap your arms around someone
Change 1 letter.

an insect
Change 1 letter.

"She wore her hair up in a ____."
Remove 1 letter.

to set something on fire
Change 1 letter.

h o r s e

b a r n

Name _____

Date _____

Castle Clan

1. Start at the bottom of the pyramid.
   Read the clues on one side. Write the
   words in the boxes.
2. Repeat on the other side.
3. Read the final clue and write the word.
   (Use the letters on the bold lines.)

Final Clue
a boy born to
a king and queen
2 letters + 4 letters

over a period
of time
"I've played the
piano _____ I was
five."
**Change 1 letter
and add 1.**

"I love to _____
that song."
**Change 1 letter
and add 1.**

to rest on a chair
Change 1 letter.

to place
"Please _____ the
box on this table."
**Remove 1 letter
and change 1.**

"Have you _____ my
other shoe?"
**Remove 1 letter
and change 1.**

q u e e n

the letters and
words in a book
Add 1 letter.

Two cups equals
one of these.
Change 1 letter.

short for
peppermint
Change 1 letter.

dislike or be
bothered by
"I don't _____ the
bad weather."
Change 1 letter.

nice and
thoughtful
Change 1 letter.

k i n g

Name _____

Date _____

Time to Learn

1. Start at the bottom of the pyramid. Read the clues on one side. Write the words in the boxes.

2. Repeat on the other side.

3. Read the final clue and write the word. (Use the letters on the bold lines.)

Final Clue
the sound of a bell
1 letter + 3 letters

This is on each side of an airplane. **Add 1 letter.**

a hairpiece **Change 1 letter.**

opposite of small **Change 1 letter.**

another word for a woman's purse **Change 1 letter.**

to ask for something again and again **Remove 1 letter and change 1.**

Foods that spoil do this. **Change 1 letter.**

a small, folding bed **Change 1 letter.**

a police officer **Remove 1 letter.**

a chicken pen **Change 1 letter.**

opposite of warm **Remove 2 letters.**

b e l l

s c h o o l

Name ______________________ Date ______________

Fruity Fun

1. Start at the bottom of the pyramid. Read the clues on one side. Write the words in the boxes.
2. Repeat on the other side.
3. Read the final clue and write the word. (Use the letters on the bold lines.)

Final Clue
a fruit that grows in bunches
2 letters + 3 letters

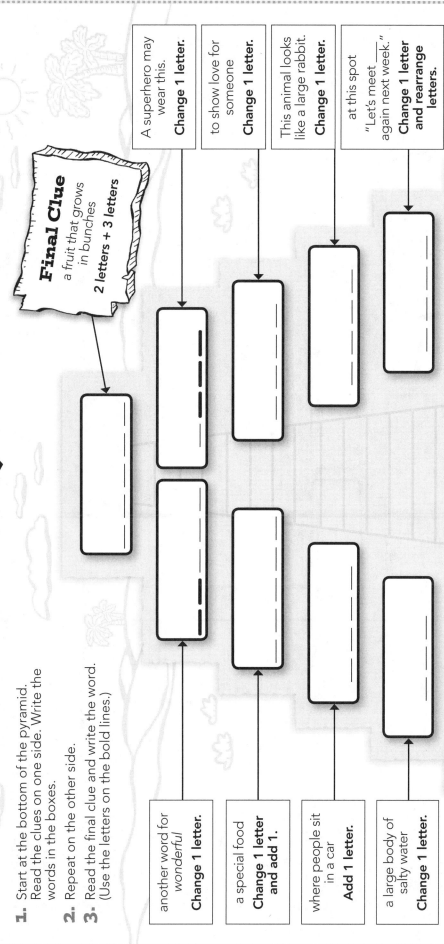

another word for *wonderful*
Change 1 letter.

a special food
Change 1 letter and add 1.

where people sit in a car
Add 1 letter.

a large body of salty water
Change 1 letter.

a tiny, round, green vegetable
Remove 2 letters.

peach

A superhero may wear this.
Change 1 letter.

to show love for someone
Change 1 letter.

This animal looks like a large rabbit.
Change 1 letter.

at this spot
"Let's meet ___ again next week."
Change 1 letter and rearrange letters.

What you do with your ears.
Change 1 letter.

pear

Name ____________________ Date ____________

Great Grooming

1. Start at the bottom of the pyramid. Read the clues on one side. Write the words in the boxes.
2. Repeat on the other side.
3. Read the final clue and write the word. (Use the letters on the bold lines.)

Final Clue
This grows on a person's head.
1 letter + 3 letters

to hold something close to you
Change 1 letter.

a floor mat
Change 1 letter.

to bother someone
"Don't ___ me while I'm reading."
Change 1 letter.

Many children ride this to school.
Remove 1 letter.

Roses grow on this.
Remove 1 letter.

b r u s h

a type of carnival
Add 1 letter.

miles and miles away
Change 1 letter.

a type of vehicle
Change 1 letter.

the place in a truck where the driver sits
Change 1 letter.

corn on the ____
Remove 1 letter.

c o m b

Name ____________________ Date ____________

A Healthy Drink

1. Start at the bottom of the pyramid. Read the clues on one side. Write the words in the boxes.
2. Repeat on the other side.
3. Read the final clue and write the word. (Use the letters on the bold lines.)

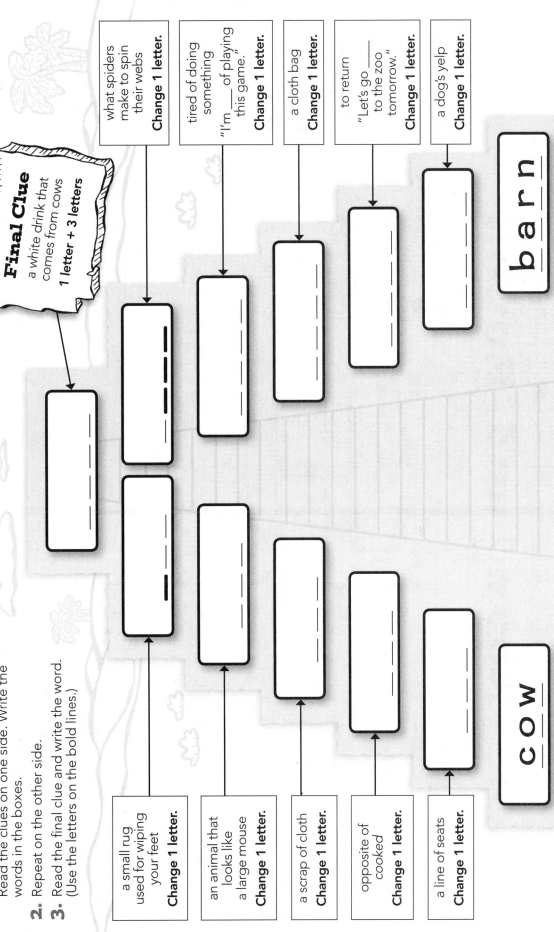

Final Clue
a white drink that comes from cows
1 letter + 3 letters

___ ___ ___ ___

a small rug used for wiping your feet
Change 1 letter.
___ ___ ___

what spiders make to spin their webs
Change 1 letter.
___ ___ ___ ___

an animal that looks like a large mouse
Change 1 letter.
___ ___ ___

tired of doing something
"I'm ___ of playing this game."
Change 1 letter.
___ ___ ___ ___

a scrap of cloth
Change 1 letter.
___ ___ ___

a cloth bag
Change 1 letter.
___ ___ ___ ___

opposite of *cooked*
Change 1 letter.
___ ___ ___

to return
"Let's go ___ to the zoo tomorrow."
Change 1 letter.
___ ___ ___ ___

a line of seats
Change 1 letter.
___ ___ ___

a dog's yelp
Change 1 letter.
___ ___ ___ ___

c o w

b a r n

Name _____ Date _____

'Round and 'Round

1. Start at the bottom of the pyramid. Read the clues on one side. Write the words in the boxes.
2. Repeat on the other side.
3. Read the final clue and write the word. (Use the letters on the bold lines.)

Final Clue
another word for twirl
2 letters + 3 letters

a tightly closed hand
Change 1 letter.

This water animal has gills and scales.
Change 1 letter.

to hope for something "I ____ I had a new bike."
Change 1 letter and add 1.

to finish a race first
Change 1 letter.

Attach a name tag to a shirt.
Remove 1 letter.

the sound a bird makes
Change 1 letter and add 1.

a dark, red vegetable that grows underground
Change 1 letter.

"Where have you ____?"
Change 1 letter.

Someone from 13 to 19 years old.
Add 1 letter.

This comes after nine.
Remove 1 letter and change 1.

s p i n

t u r n

Measure Me

Name _____   Date _____

1. Start at the bottom of the pyramid. Read the clues on one side. Write the words in the boxes.
2. Repeat on the other side.
3. Read the final clue and write the word. (Use the letters on the bold lines.)

Final Clue
a three-foot-long stick used for measuring
1 letter + 3 letters

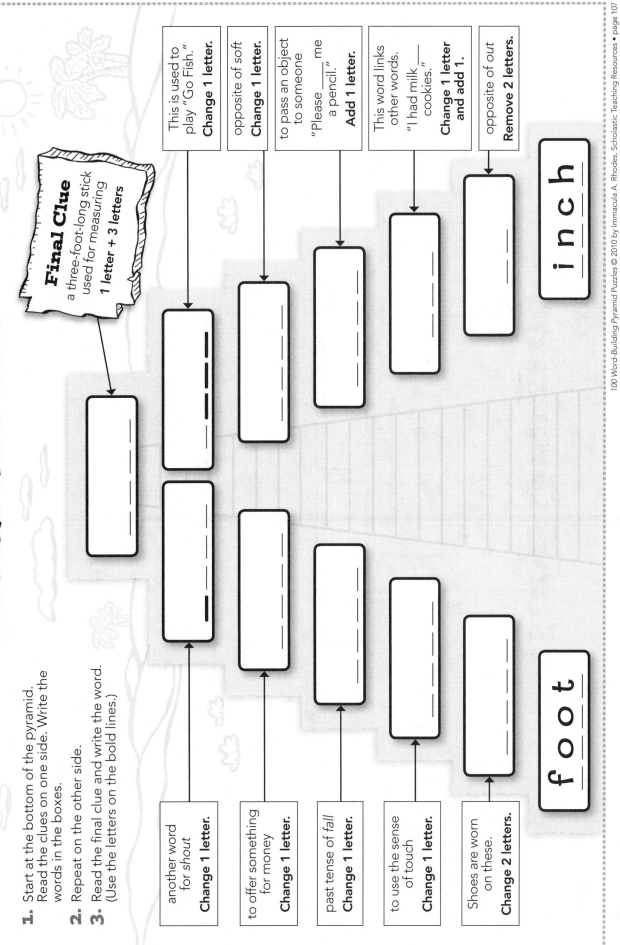

This is used to play "Go Fish." **Change 1 letter.**

opposite of soft **Change 1 letter.**

to pass an object to someone "Please ____ me a pencil." **Add 1 letter.**

This word links other words. "I had milk ____ cookies." **Change 1 letter and add 1.**

opposite of out **Remove 2 letters.**

i n c h

another word for shout **Change 1 letter.**

to offer something for money **Change 1 letter.**

past tense of fall **Change 1 letter.**

to use the sense of touch **Change 1 letter.**

Shoes are worn on these. **Change 2 letters.**

f o o t

Name ____________________ Date ____________

Good Grazing

1. Start at the bottom of the pyramid. Read the clues on one side. Write the words in the boxes.
2. Repeat on the other side.
3. Read the final clue and write the word. (Use the letters on the bold lines.)

Final Clue
opposite of *thin*
2 letters + 3 letters

___ ___ ___ ___ ___

"____ you for the birthday gift."
Change 1 letter and add 1.

___ ___ ___ ___ ___

People keep their money in this.
Change 1 letter.

___ ___ ___ ___

a group that plays music
Add 1 letter.

___ ___ ___ ___

another word for *terrible*
Remove 1 letter and change 1.

___ ___ ___

a type of fish
Remove 1 letter and change 1.

___ ___ ___ ___

g r a s s

to pull an apple off a tree
Remove 1 letter and change 1.

___ ___ ___ ___

the sound computer keys make
Change 1 letter.

___ ___ ___ ___ ___

This is used for telling time.
Change 1 letter and add 1.

___ ___ ___ ___ ___

a large stone
Change 1 letter and add 1.

___ ___ ___ ___

A person uses oars to ___ a boat.
Remove 1 letter.

___ ___ ___

g r o w

Answer Key

Furry Friends, *page 8*
top: pet
left: dog, log, leg, peg
right: cat, cut, nut, net

Sweet Spread, *page 9*
top: lid
left: jar, car, cap, lap
right: jam, ram, rim, rid

Catching Critters, *page 10*
top: jar
left: net, pet, set, jet
right: bug, bag, bar, far

Special Delivery, *page 11*
top: mail
left: stamp, camp, cap, map
right: send, sand, said, sail

Made by Hand, *page 12*
top: cut
left: glue, clue, club, cub
right: fold, gold, got, gut

The Upper Level, *page 13*
top: neck
left: head, heal, hear, near
right: chest, pest, peak, peck

On the Water, *page 14*
top: sail
left: lake, cake, cave, save
right: boat, bat, bait, bail

A Nice Day Out, *page 15*
top: rest
left: park, bark, bare, rare
right: bench, bend, bent, best

Going for a Walk, *page 16*
top: park
left: trail, rail, rain, pain
right: hike, bike, bake, bark

Running Around, *page 17*
top: mouse
left: cat, bat, mat, mate
right: chase, chose, hose, house

At the Game, *page 18*
top: pitch
left: ball, hall, hill, pill
right: catch, match, hatch, hitch

Little One, *page 19*
top: child
left: boy, toy, top, chop
right: girl, gill, will, wild

At the Door, *page 20*
top: close
left: slam, slim, slip, clip
right: shut, hut, hot, hose

Fun Figures, *page 21*
top: shape
left: heart, hear, her, she
right: square, care, cape, tape

Colorful Words, *page 22*
top: green
left: red, fed, few, grew
right: blue, bee, see, seen

Underfoot, *page 23*
top: ground
left: rock, row, crow, grow
right: soil, foil, foul, found

Signs of the Season, *page 24*
top: fall
left: leaf, lean, bean, can, fan
right: wind, wand, band, bald, ball

Coin Keeper, *page 25*
top: save
left: bank, tank, tan, ton, son
right: dime, lime, lame, game, gave

A Great Story, *page 26*
top: read
left: page, pale, pal, pat, rat
right: book, look, leak, beak, bead

On the Road, *page 27*
top: trip
left: bag, tag, rag, rash, trash
right: bus, bud, bid, hid, hip

Batter Up!, *page 28*
top: base
left: glove, love, live, like, bike
right: ball, fall, fake, cake, case

Let's Go Out!, *page 29*
top: coat
left: boot, hoot, hook, book, cook
right: scarf, car, oar, oat, boat

Flapping and Flying, *page 30*
top: wave
left: flag, lag, bag, big, wig
right: pole, pale, page, pave, gave

Put It on Paper, *page 31*
top: write
left: hand, sand, sang, song, wrong
right: pen, pin, pit, kit, kite

On the Go!, *page 32*
top: move
left: push, bush, rush, rust, must
right: pull, put, pot, lot, love

On Your Feet, *page 33*
top: stand
left: walk, wall, tall, tale, stale
right: run, ran, rang, hang, hand

Shade Maker, *page 34*
top: tree
left: limb, lamb, lamp, lap, trap
right: leaf, lead, bead, bed, bee

In the Water, *page 35*
top: swim
left: fish, wish, will, well, swell
right: sea, seal, deal, dial, dim

Living in the Wild, *page 36*
top: bear
left: cub, tub, tug, rug, bug
right: cave, care, car, tar, tear

Sun Up, Sun Down, *page 37*
top: sleep
left: wake, lake, lame, lime, slime
right: bed, fed, need, weed, weep

Food Farm, *page 38*
top: crop
left: bean, beat, beet, beep, creep
right: corn, born, torn, ton, top

Fun With a Friend, *page 39*
top: play
left: game, gate, date, late, plate
right: turn, burn, born, boy, say

Up We Go!, *page 40*
top: stair
left: climb, limb, limp, lamp, stamp
right: rail, sail, tail, fail, fair

In the Flowerpot, *page 41*
top: grow
left: plant, pant, pan, pin, grin
right: soil, oil, owl, bowl, bow

At the Store, *page 42*
top: spend
left: coin, cot, dot, pot, spot
right: buy, bug, beg, bed, bend

Hungry Hound, *page 43*
top: dog
left: bone, tone, ton, ten, den
right: bark, bar, bag, hug, hog

Time Out, *page 44*
top: cot
left: rest, best, bet, but, cut
right: nap, map, mop, hop, hot

Tree Topper, *page 45*
top: nest
left: bird, bind, mind, mine, nine
right: tree, fee, felt, belt, best

Chugging Along, *page 46*
top: track
left: rail, raid, rid, rip, trip
right: train, rain, ran, pan, pack

Check the Calendar, *page 47*
top: year
left: week, weed, wee, wet, yet
right: day, dad, dead, dear, near

Say "Cheese!", *page 48*
top: smile
left: brush, rush, rash, mash, smash
right: teeth, teen, tee, tie, tile

Spending the Day Away, *page 49*
top: mall
left: shop, shot, not, net, met
right: store, stare, star, stall, tall

That Makes Sense!, *page 50*
top: smell
left: hear, ear, star, start, smart
right: taste, waste, was, wall, well

Scrub-a-Dub-Dub, *page 51*
top: hand
left: wash, mash, mast, mat, hat
right: soap, soak, sock, sack, sand

Look-Alikes, *page 52*
top: match
left: twin, win, fin, find, mind
right: pair, pail, pal, pat, patch

Time to Cook, *page 53*
top: blend
left: stir, steer, steep, seep, bleed
right: mix, six, sit, set, send

Dark to Light, *page 54*
top: white
left: gray, ray, may, my, why
right: black, back, bat, bit, bite

Frozen Fun, *page 55*
top: skate
left: glide, wide, win, kin, skin
right: ice, mice, rice, race, rate

Happy Times, *page 56*
top: glad
left: grin, grow, blow, blue, glue
right: smile, mile, male, made, mad

Surprise!, *page 57*
top: gift
left: box, bow, tow, town, gown
right: lid, lip, lit, list, lift

Squirrel's Lunch, *page 58*
top: shell
left: nut, put, pot, hot, shot
right: crack, back, buck, bull, bell

Mmm, Mmm, Good!, *page 59*
top: boil
left: pot, post, past, pest, best
right: soup, sour, four, foul, foil

Wet Weather, *page 60*
top: rain
left: cloud, loud, load, toad, road
right: storm, store, stare, stair, stain

Under Construction, *page 61*
top: nail
left: build, bud, bed, bet, net
right: wood, food, fool, foil, fail

Safe and Sound, *page 62*
top: lock
left: key, cry, crab, cab, lab
right: door, poor, pool, tool, tock

Breakin' Out, *page 63*
top: chick
left: egg, peg, pig, pin, chin
right: crack, rack, back, sack, sick

Size It Up, *page 64*
top: wide
left: long, lone, lane, land, wand
right: tall, tale, tame, time, tide

Picture Perfect, *page 65*
top: draw
left: paint, pint, hint, hip, drip
right: art, ant, pant, pat, paw

Take Action, *page 66*
top: quick
left: slow, low, lot, lit, quit
right: move, love, live, like, lick

At the Seashore, *page 67*
top: beach
left: crab, crash, cash, case, base
right: clam, cram, cream, read, reach

Steppin' Out, *page 68*
top: foot
left: sock, sick, sink, pink, pin, fin
right: shoe, show, how, hot, rot, root

Where Can It Be?, *page 69*
top: find
left: look, lock, lick, sick, sit, fit
right: lost, most, mist, mitt, mint, mind

Freshwater Friends, *page 70*
top: pond
left: frog, fog, log, leg, let, pet
right: fish, fist, fit, fin, find, fond

Moving Along, *page 71*
top: snake
left: slide, slip, clip, clap, slap, snap
right: grass, pass, past, paste, waste, wake

Are You Thirsty?, *page 72*
top: drink
left: cup, cap, tap, tag, rag, drag
right: mouth, out, put, pit, pin, pink

It's Wintertime!, *page 73*
top: snow
left: cold, hold, hole, hop, hip, snip
right: flake, lake, lawn, law, low, mow

Growing Up, *page 74*
top: plant
left: stem, step, stop, top, pop, plop
right: root, rot, pot, pat, pan, pant

At School, *page 75*
top: teach
left: learn, lead, bead, bad, bar, tar
right: class, pass, pat, eat, each, peach

Flying High, *page 76*
top: string
left: tail, rain, raid, rap, trap, strap
right: kite, kit, fit, fin, win, wing

Sip It Up, *page 77*
top: straw
left: lid, hid, had, hay, tray, stray
right: cup, cap, lap, lab, law, claw

In the Cafeteria, *page 78*
top: meal
left: lunch, bunch, bun, fun, fan, man
right: eat, neat, beat, seat, seal, real

Good for You, *page 79*
top: treat
left: fruit, suit, sit, sip, rip, trip
right: snack, stack, sack, sat, eat, heat

Baby Bird, *page 80*
top: fly
left: wing, win, fin, fit, fat, flat
right: flap, lap, lip, rip, trip, try

Pump and Pedal, *page 81*
top: bike
left: ride, wide, hide, hid, had, bad
right: tire, fire, fare, fake, lake, like

Happy Tune, *page 82*
top: song
left: clap, cap, car, far, fat, sat
right: beat, bear, boar, bone, lone, long

Taking a Drive, *page 83*
top: road
left: wheel, heel, feel, fee, fed, red
right: car, can, man, moan, loan, load

Turn It On, *page 84*
top: light
left: shade, share, hare, hate, mate, late
right: lamp, limp, lip, sip, sit, sight

Time to Eat!, *page 85*
top: spoon
left: plate, late, lace, race, pace, space
right: fork, work, word, wood, mood, moon

24 Hours, *page 86*
top: clock
left: time, tame, tape, tap, lap, clap
right: tick, pick, pack, back, sack, sock

In the Dark Sky, *page 87*
top: night
left: fly, flea, tea, pea, pear, near
right: bat, bit, big, dig, fig, fight

Waddling Along, *page 88*
top: duck
left: bird, bind, mind, mine, line, dine
right: quack, tack, rack, rock, lock, luck

On a Lily Pad, *page 89*
top: frog
left: leap, lap, slap, sly, fly, fry
right: hop, cop, cot, lot, dot, dog

Outer Space, *page 90*
top: star
left: moon, moan, man, mall, tall, stall
right: sun, fun, fan, far, bar, car

Feathery Swimmer, *page 91*
top: quack
left: duck, luck, lick, lit, fit, quit
right: bill, bell, belt, bet, bat, back

In the Ground, *page 92*
top: soil
left: worm, wore, more, mole, male, sale
right: dig, big, bill, ball, bail, boil

Around the Barn, *page 93*
top: farm
left: cow, tow, ton, son, sun, fun
right: pig, wig, wag, war, warm, harm

At Work, *page 94*
top: chair
left: desk, dusk, dust, bust, best, chest
right: seat, sat, pat, pad, paid, pair

Up on Top, *page 95*
top: head
left: hat, pat, part, cart, card, hard
right: hair, fair, far, fear, dear, dead

The Great Outdoors, *page 96*
top: sea
left: land, hand, had, hat, hit, sit
right: sky, say, sat, pat, pet, pea

On the Map, *page 97*
top: state
left: city, pity, pit, pick, tick, stick
right: town, down, dawn, dart, dare, date

Twinkle, Twinkle, *page 98*
top: bright
left: star, stir, sir, sing, ring, bring
right: shine, fine, fin, fit, fig, fight

Warm and Toasty, *page 99*
top: wood
left: fire, wire, tire, hire, here, were
right: burn, bun, sun, soon, moon, mood

Saddle Up!, *page 100*
top: ride
left: barn, burn, bun, bug, hug, rug
right: horse, hoe, toe, tie, time, tide

Castle Clan, *page 101*
top: prince
left: king, kind, mind, mint, pint, print
right: queen, seen, set, sit, sing, since

Time to Learn, *page 102*
top: ring
left: school, cool, coop, cop, cot, rot
right: bell, beg, bag, big, wig, wing

Fruity Fun, *page 103*
top: grape
left: peach, pea, sea, seat, treat, great
right: pear, hear, here, hare, care, cape

Great Grooming, *page 104*
top: hair
left: brush, bush, bus, bug, rug, hug
right: comb, cob, cab, car, far, fair

A Healthy Drink, *page 105*
top: milk
left: cow, row, raw, rag, rat, mat
right: barn, bark, back, sack, sick, silk

'Round and 'Round, *page 106*
top: twist
left: turn, ten, teen, been, beet, tweet
right: spin, pin, win, wish, fish, fist

Measure Me, *page 107*
top: yard
left: foot, feet, feel, fell, sell, yell
right: inch, in, and, hand, hard, card

Good Grazing, *page 108*
top: thick
left: grass, bass, bad, band, bank, thank
right: grow, row, rock, clock, click, pick